THE IDEA (...)
BY MODERN KNOWLEDGE

By JOHN FISKE

Fourteenth Thousand

BOSTON AND NEW YORK
HOUGHTON, MIFFLIN AND COMPANY
The Riverside Press, Cambridge
1893

Copyright, 1885,
By JOHN FISKE.

All rights reserved.

The *Riverside Press*, Cambridge, Mass., U.S.A.
Electrotyped and Printed by H. O. Houghton & Company.

To

MY WIFE,

IN REMEMBRANCE OF THE SWEET SUNDAY MORNING

UNDER THE APPLE-TREE ON THE HILLSIDE,

WHEN WE TWO SAT LOOKING DOWN INTO FAIRY WOODLAND PATHS,

AND TALKED OF THE THINGS

SINCE WRITTEN IN THIS LITTLE BOOK,

I now dedicate it.

Ἀργύριον καὶ χρυσίον οὐχ ὑπάρχει
μοι· ὃ δὲ ἔχω, τοῦτό σοι δίδωμι.

PREFACE.

WHEN asked to give a second address before the Concord School of Philosophy, I gladly accepted the invitation, as affording a proper occasion for saying certain things which I had for some time wished to say about theism. My address was designed to introduce the discussion of the question whether pantheism is the legitimate outcome of modern science. It seemed to me that the object might best be attained by passing in review the various modifications which the idea of God has undergone in the past, and pointing out the shape in which it is likely to survive the rapid growth of modern knowledge, and especially the establishment of that great doctrine of evolution which is fast obliging us to revise our opinions upon all subjects whatsoever. Having thus in the text outlined the idea of God most likely to be conceived by minds trained in the doctrine of evolution, I left it for further discussion to decide whether the term "pantheism" can properly be applied to such a conception. While much enlightenment may be got from carefully describing the substance of a philosophic doctrine, very little can be gained by merely affixing to it a label; and I could not but feel that my argument would be simply encumbered by the introduction of any question of nomenclature involving such a vague and uninstructive epithet as "pantheism." Such epithets are often regarded with favour and freely used, as seeming to obviate the necessity for that kind of labour to which most people are most averse, — the labour of sustained and accurate thinking. People are too apt to make such general terms do duty in place of a careful examination of facts, and are thus sometimes led to strange conclusions. When, for example, they have heard somebody called an "agnostic," they at once think they know all about him; whereas they have very likely learned nothing that is of the slightest value in characterizing his opinions or his mental attitude. A term that can be applied at once to a Comte, a Mansel, and a Huxley is obviously of little use in the matter of definition. But, it may be asked, in spite of their world-wide differences, do not these three thinkers agree in holding that nothing can be known about the nature of God? Perhaps so, — one cannot answer even this plain question with an unqualified yes; but, granting that they fully agree in this assertion of ignorance, nevertheless, in their philosophic attitudes with regard to this ignorance, in the use they severally make of the assertion, in the way it determines their inferences about all manner of other things, the differences are so vast that nothing but mental confusion can come from a terminology which would content itself by applying to all three the common epithet "agnostic." The case is similar with such a word as "pantheism," which has been familiarly applied to so many utterly diverse systems of thought that it is very hard to tell just what it means. It has been equally applied to the doctrine of "the Hindu philosophers of the orthodox Brahmanical schools," who "hold that all finite existence is an illusion, and life mere vexation and mistake, a blunder or sorry jest of the Absolute;" and to the doctrine of the Stoics, who "went to the other extreme, and held that the universe was the product of perfect reason and in an absolute sense good." (Pollock's "Spinoza," p. 356.) In recent times it has been commonly used as a vituperative epithet, and hurled indiscriminately at such unpopular opinions as do not seem to call for so heavy a missile as the more cruel term "atheism." The writer who sets forth in plain scientific language a physical theory of the universe is liable to be scowled at and called an atheist; but, when the very same ideas are presented in the form of oracular apophthegm or poetic rhapsody, the author is more gently described as "tinctured with pantheism."

But out of the chaos of vagueness in which this unhappy word has been immersed it is perhaps still possible to extract something like a definite meaning. In the broadest sense there are three possible ways in which we may contemplate the universe.

First, we may regard the world of phenomena as sufficient unto itself, and deny that it needs to be referred to any underlying and all-comprehensive unity. Nothing has an ultimate origin or destiny; there is no dramatic tendency in the succession of events, nor any ultimate law to which everything must be referred; there is no reasonableness in the universe save that with which human fancy unwarrantably endows it; the events of the world have no orderly progression like the scenes of a well-constructed plot, but in the manner of their coming and going they constitute simply what Chauncey Wright so aptly called "cosmical weather;" they drift and eddy about in an utterly blind and irrational manner, though now and then evolving, as if by accident, temporary combinations which have to us a rational appearance. This is Atheism, pure and unqualified. It recognizes no Omnipresent Energy.

Secondly, we may hold that the world of phenomena is utterly unintelligible unless referred to an underlying and all-comprehensive unity. All things are manifestations of an Omnipresent Energy which cannot be in any imaginable sense personal or anthropomorphic; out from this eternal source of phenomena all individualities proceed, and into it they must all ultimately return and be absorbed; the events of the world have an orderly progression, but not toward any goal recognizable by us; in the process of evolution there is nothing that from any point of view can be called teleological; the beginning and end of things — that which is Alpha and Omega — is merely an inscrutable essence, a formless void. Such a view as this may properly be called Pantheism. It recognizes an Omnipresent Energy, but virtually identifies it with the totality of things.

Thirdly, we may hold that the world of phenomena is intelligible only when regarded as the multiform manifestation of an Omnipresent Energy that is in some way — albeit in a way quite above our finite comprehension — anthropomorphic or quasi-personal. There is a true objective reasonableness in the universe; its events have an orderly progression, and, so far as those events are brought sufficiently within our ken for us to generalize them exhaustively, their progression is toward a goal that is recognizable by human intelligence; "the process of evolution is itself the working out of a mighty Teleology of which our finite understandings can fathom but the scantiest rudiments" ("Cosmic Philosophy," vol. ii. p. 406); it is indeed but imperfectly that we can describe the dramatic tendency in the succession of events, but we can see enough to assure us of the fundamental fact that there is such a tendency; and this tendency is the objective aspect of that which, when regarded on its subjective side, we call Purpose. Such a theory of things is Theism. It recognizes an Omnipresent Energy, which is none other than the living God.

It is this theistic doctrine which I hold myself, and which in the present essay I have sought to exhibit as the legitimate outcome of modern scientific thought. I was glad to have such an excellent occasion for returning to the subject as the invitation from Concord gave me, because in a former attempt to expound the same doctrine I do not seem to have succeeded in making myself understood. In my

"Outlines of Cosmic Philosophy," published in 1874, I endeavoured to set forth a theory of theism identical with that which is set forth in the present essay. But an acute and learned friend, writing under the pseudonym of "Physicus," in his "Candid Examination of Theism" (London, 1878), thus criticizes my theory: In it, he says, "while I am able to discern the elements which I think may properly be regarded as common to Theism and to Atheism, I am not able to discern any single element that is specifically distinctive of Theism" (p. 145). The reason for the inability of "Physicus" to discern any such specifically distinctive element is that he misunderstands me as proposing to divest the theistic idea of every shred of anthropomorphism, while still calling it a theistic idea. This, he thinks, would be an utterly illegitimate proceeding, and I quite agree with him. In similar wise my friend Mr. Frederick Pollock, in his admirable work on Spinoza (London, 1880), observes that "Mr. Fiske's doctrine excludes the belief in a so-called Personal God, and the particular forms of religious emotion dependent on it" (p. 356). If the first part of this sentence stood alone, I might pause to inquire how much latitude of meaning may be conveyed in the expression "so-called;" is it meant that I exclude the belief in a Personal God as it was held by Augustine and Paley, or as it was held by Clement and Schleiermacher, or both? But the second clause of the sentence seems to furnish the answer; it seems to imply that I would practically do away with Theism altogether.

Such a serious misstatement of my position, made in perfect good faith by two thinkers so conspicuous for ability and candour, shows that, in spite of all the elaborate care with which the case was stated in "Cosmic Philosophy," some further explanation is needed. It is true that there are expressions in that work which, taken singly and by themselves, might seem to

Preface.

imply a total rejection of theism. Such expressions occur chiefly in the chapter entitled "Anthropomorphic Theism," where great pains are taken to show the inadequacy of the Paley argument from design, and to point out the insuperable difficulties in which we are entangled by the conception of a Personal God as it is held by the great majority of modern theologians who have derived it from Plato and Augustine. In the succeeding chapters, however, it is expressly argued that the total elimination of anthropomorphism from the idea of God is impossible. There are some who, recognizing that the ideas of Personality and Infinity are unthinkable in combination, seek to escape the difficulty by speaking of God as the "Infinite Power;" that is, instead of a symbol derived from our notion of human consciousness, they employ a symbol derived from our notion of force in general. For many philosophic purposes the device is eminently useful; but it should not be forgotten that, while the form of our experience of Personality does not allow us to conceive it as infinite, it is equally true that the form of our experience of Force does not allow us to conceive it as infinite, since we know force only as antagonized by other force. Since, moreover, our notion of force is purely a generalization from our subjective sensations of effort overcoming resistance, there is scarcely less anthropomorphism lurking in the phrase "Infinite Power" than in the phrase "Infinite Person." Now in "Cosmic Philosophy" I argue that the presence of God is the one all-pervading fact of life, from which there is no escape; that while in the deepest sense the nature of Deity is unknowable by finite Man, nevertheless the exigencies of our thinking oblige us to symbolize that nature in some form that has a real meaning for us; and that we cannot symbolize that nature as in any wise physical, but are bound to symbolize it as in some way psychical. I do not here repeat the arguments, but simply state the conclusions. The final conclusion (vol. ii. p 449) is that we must not say that "God is Force," since such a phrase inevitably calls up those pantheistic notions of blind necessity, which it is my express desire to avoid; but, always bearing in mind the symbolic character of the words, we may say that "God is Spirit." How my belief in the personality of God could be more strongly expressed without entirely deserting the language of modern philosophy and taking refuge in pure mythology, I am unable to see

There are two points in the present essay which I hope will serve to define more completely the kind of theism which I have tried to present as compatible with the doctrine of evolution. One is the historic contrast between anthropomorphic and cosmic theism regarded in their modes of genesis, and especially as exemplified within the Christian church in the very different methods and results of Augustine on the one hand and Athanasius on the other. The view which I have ventured to designate as "cosmic theism" is no invention of mine; in its most essential features it has been entertained by some of the profoundest thinkers of Christendom in ancient and modern times, from Clement of Alexandria to Lessing and Goethe and Schleiermacher. The other point is the teleological inference drawn from the argument of my first Concord address on "The Destiny of Man, viewed in the Light of his Origin."

When that address was published, a year ago, I was surprised to find it quite commonly regarded as indicating some radical change of attitude on my part, — a "conversion," perhaps, from one set of opinions to another. Inasmuch as the argument in the "Destiny of Man" was based in every one of its parts upon arguments already published in "Cosmic Philosophy" (1874), and in the "Unseen World" (1876), I naturally could not understand why the later book should impress people so differently from the earlier ones. It presently appeared, however, that none of my friends who had studied the earlier books had detected any such change of attitude ; it was only people who knew little or nothing about me, or else the newspapers. Whence the inference seemed obvious that many readers of the "Destiny of Man" must have contrasted it, not with my earlier books which they had not read, but with some vague and distorted notion about my views which had grown up (Heaven knows how or why!) through the medium of "the press;" and thus there might have been produced the impression that those views had undergone a radical change.

It would be little to my credit, however, had my views of the doctrine of evolution and its implications undergone no development or enlargement since the publication of "Cosmic Philosophy." To carry such a subject about in one's mind for ten years, without having any new thoughts about it, would hardly be a proof of fitness for philosophizing. I have for some time been aware of a shortcoming in the earlier work, which it is the purpose of these two Concord addresses in some measure to remedy. That shortcoming was an imperfect appreciation of the goal toward which the process of evolution is tending, and a consequent failure to state adequately how the doctrine of evolution must affect our estimate of Man's place in Nature. Nothing of fundamental importance in "Cosmic Philosophy" needed changing, but a new chapter needed to be written, in order to show how the doctrine of evolution, by exhibiting the development of the highest spiritual human qualities as the goal toward which God's creative work has from the outset been tending, replaces Man in his old position of headship in the universe, even as in the days of Dante and Aquinas. That which the pre-Copernican astronomy naively thought to do by placing the home of Man in the centre of the physical universe, the Darwinian biology profoundly accomplishes by exhibiting Man as the terminal fact in that stupendous process of evolution whereby things have come to be what they are. In the deepest sense it is as true as it ever was held to be, that the world was made for Man, and that the bringing forth in him of those qualities which we call highest and holiest is the final cause of creation. The arguments upon which this conclusion rests, as they are set forth in the "Destiny of Man" and epitomized in the concluding section of the present essay, may all be found in "Cosmic Philosophy;" but I failed to sum them up there and indicate the conclusion, almost within reach, which I had not quite clearly seized. When, after long hovering in the background of consciousness, it suddenly flashed upon me two years ago, it came with such vividness as to seem like a revelation.

This conclusion as to the implications of the doctrine of evolution concerning

Man's place in Nature supplies the element wanting in the theistic theory set forth in "Cosmic Philosophy," — the teleological element. It is profoundly true that a theory of things may seem theistic or atheistic in virtue of what it says of Man, no less than in virtue of what it says of God. The craving for a final cause is so deeply rooted in human nature that no doctrine of theism which fails to satisfy it can seem other than lame and ineffective. In writing "Cosmic Philosophy" I fully realized this when, in the midst of the argument against Paley's form of theism, I said that "the process of evolution is itself the working out of a mighty Teleology of which our finite understandings can fathom but the scantiest rudiments." Nevertheless, while the whole momentum of my thought carried me to the conviction that it must be so, I was not yet able to indicate *how* it is so, and I accordingly left the subject with this brief and inadequate hint. Could the point have been worked out then and there, I think it would have left no doubt in the minds of "Physicus" and Mr. Pollock as to the true character of Cosmic Theism.

But hold, cries the scientific inquirer, what in the world are you doing? Are we again to resuscitate the phantom Teleology, which we had supposed at last safely buried between cross-roads and pinned down with a stake? Was not Bacon right in characterizing "final causes" as vestal virgins, so barren has their study proved? And has not Huxley, with yet keener sarcasm, designated them the *hetairæ* of philosophy, so often have they led men astray? Very true. I do not wish to take back a single word of all that I have said in my chapter on "Anthropomorphic Theism" in condemnation of the teleological method and the peculiar theistic doctrines upon which it rests. As a means of investigation it is absolutely worthless. Nay, it is worse than worthless; it is treacherous, it is debauching to the intellect. But that is no reason why, when a distinct dramatic tendency in the events of the universe appears as the *result* of purely scientific investigation, we should refuse to recognize it. It is the object of the "Destiny of Man" to prove that there is such a dramatic tendency; and while such a tendency cannot be regarded as indicative of purpose in the limited anthropomorphic sense, it is still, as I said before, the objective aspect of that which, when regarded on its subjective side, we call Purpose. There is a reasonableness in the universe such as to indicate that the Infinite Power of which it is the multiform manifestation is psychical, though it is impossible to ascribe to Him any of the limited psychical attributes which we know, or to argue from the ways of Man to the ways of God. For, as St. Paul reminds us, "who hath known the mind of the Lord, or who hath been his counsellor?"

It is in this sense that I accept Mr.

Spencer's doctrine of the Unknowable. How far my interpretation agrees with his own I do not undertake to say. On such an abstruse matter it is best that one should simply speak for one's self. But in his recent essay on "Retrogressive Religion" he uses expressions which imply a doctrine of theism essentially similar to that here maintained. The "infinite and eternal Energy from which all things proceed," and which is the same power that "in ourselves wells up under the form of consciousness," is certainly the power which is here recognized as God. The term "Unknowable" I have carefully refrained from using; it does not occur in the text of this essay. It describes only one aspect of Deity, but it has been seized upon by shallow writers of every school, treated as if fully synonymous with Deity, and made the theme of the most dismal twaddle that the world has been deluged with since the days of mediæval scholasticism. The latest instance is the wretched positivist rubbish which Mr. Frederic Harrison has mistaken for criticism, and to which it is almost a pity that Mr. Spencer should have felt called upon to waste his valuable time in replying. That which Mr. Spencer throughout all his works regards as the All-Being, the Power of which "our lives, alike physical and mental, in common with all the activities, organic and inorganic, amid which we live, are but the workings," — this omnipresent Power it pleases Mr. Harrison to call the "All-Nothingness," to describe it as "a logical formula begotten in controversy, dwelling apart from man and the world" (whatever all that may mean), and to imagine its worshippers as thus addressing it in prayer, "O x^n, love us, help us, make us one with thee!" If Mr. Harrison's aim were to understand, rather than to misrepresent, the religious attitude which goes with such a conception of Deity as Mr. Spencer's, he could nowhere find it more happily expressed than in these wonderful lines of Goethe : —

"Weltseele, komm, uns zu durchdringen!
Dann mit dem Weltgeist selbst zu ringen
 Wird unsrer Kräfte Hochberuf.
Theilnehmend führen gute Geister,
Gelinde leitend, höchste Meister,
 Zu dem der alles schafft und schuf."

Mr. Harrison is enabled to perform his antics simply because he happens to have such a word as "Unknowable" to play with. Yet the word which has been put to such unseemly uses is, when properly understood, of the highest value in theistic philosophy. That Deity *per se* is not only unknown but unknowable is a truth which Mr. Spencer has illustrated with all the resources of that psychologic analysis of which he is incomparably the greatest master the world has ever seen; but it is not a truth which originated with him, or the demonstration of which is tantamount, as Mr. Harrison would have us believe, to the destruction of all religion. Among all the Christian theologians that have lived, there are few higher names than Athanasius, who also regarded Deity *per se* as unknowable, being revealed to mankind only through incarnation in Christ. It is not as failing to recognize its value that I have refrained in this essay from using the term "Unknowable;" it is because so many false and stupid inferences have been drawn from Mr. Spencer's use of the word that it seemed worth while to show how a doctrine essentially similar to his might be expounded without introducing it. For further elucidation I will simply repeat in this connection what I wrote long ago: "It is enough to remind the reader that Deity is unknowable just in so far as it is not manifested to consciousness through the phenomenal world, — knowable just in so far as it is thus manifested: unknowable in so far as infinite and absolute, — knowable in the order of its phenomenal manifestations; knowable, in a symbolic way, as the Power which is disclosed in every throb of the mighty rhythmic life of the universe; knowable as the eternal Source of a Moral

Law which is implicated with each action of our lives, and in obedience to which lies our only guaranty of the happiness which is incorruptible, and which neither inevitable misfortune nor unmerited obloquy can take away. Thus, though we may not by searching find out God, though we may not compass infinitude or attain to absolute knowledge, we may at least know all that it concerns us to know, as intelligent and responsible beings. They who seek to know more than this, to transcend the conditions under which alone is knowledge possible, are, in Goethe's profound language, as wise as little children who, when they have looked into a mirror, turn it around to see what is behind it. ("Cosmic Philosophy," vol. ii. p. 470.)

The present essay must be regarded as a sequel to the "Destiny of Man," — so much so that the force of the argument in the concluding section can hardly be appreciated without reference to the other book. The two books, taken together, contain the bare outlines of a theory of religion which I earnestly hope at some future time to state elaborately in a work on the true nature of Christianity. Some such scheme had begun vaguely to dawn upon my mind when I was fourteen years old, and thought in the language of the rigid Calvinistic orthodoxy then prevalent in New England. After many and extensive changes of opinion, the idea assumed definite shape in the autumn of 1869, when I conceived the plan of a book to be entitled "Jesus of Nazareth and the Founding of Christianity," — a work intended to deal on the one hand with the natural genesis of the complex aggregate of beliefs and aspirations known as Christianity, and on the other hand with the metamorphoses which are being wrought in this aggregate by modern knowledge and modern theories of the universe. Such a book, involving a treatment both historical and philosophical, requires long and varied preparation; and I have always regarded my other books, published from time to time, as simply wayside studies preliminary to the undertaking of this complicated and difficult task. While thus habitually shaping my work with reference to this cherished idea, I have written some things which are in a special sense related to it. The rude outlines of a very small portion of the historical treatment are contained in the essays on "The Jesus of History," and "The Christ of Dogma," published in the volume entitled "The Unseen World, and Other Essays." The outlines of the philosophical treatment are partially set forth in the "Destiny of Man" and in the present work.

It amused me to see that almost every review of the "Destiny of Man" took pains to state that it was my Concord address "rewritten and expanded." Such trifles help one to understand the helter-skelter way in which more important things get said and believed. The "Destiny of

Man" was printed exactly as it was delivered at Concord, without the addition, or subtraction, or alteration of a single word. The case is the same with the present work.

PETERSHAM, *September 6, 1885.*

CONTENTS.

I. Difficulty of expressing the Idea of God so that it can be readily understood . . . 35
II. The Rapid Growth of Modern Knowledge . 46
III. Sources of the Theistic Idea 62
IV. Development of Monotheism 72
V. The Idea of God as immanent in the World . 81
VI. The Idea of God as remote from the World . 87
VII. Conflict between the Two Ideas, commonly misunderstood as a Conflict between Religion and Science 97
VIII. Anthropomorphic Conceptions of God . . 111
IX. The Argument from Design 118
X. Simile of the Watch replaced by Simile of the Flower 128
XI. The Craving for a Final Cause 134
XII. Symbolic Conceptions 140
XIII. The Eternal Source of Phenomena . . . 144
XIV. The Power that makes for Righteousness . 158

THE IDEA OF GOD.

I.

Difficulty of expressing the Idea of God so that it can be readily understood.

IN Goethe's great poem, while Faust is walking with Margaret at eventide in the garden, she asks him questions about his religion. It is long since he has been shriven or attended mass; does he, then, believe in God? — a question easy to answer with a simple yes, were it not for the form in which it is put. The great scholar and subtle thinker, who has delved in the deepest mines of philosophy and come forth weary and heavy-laden with their boasted treasures, has framed a very different conception of God from that entertained by the priest at the confessional or the altar, and how is he to make this intelligible to the simple-minded girl that walks by his side? Who will make bold to declare that he can grasp an idea of such overwhelming vastness as the idea of God, yet who that hath the feelings of a man can bring himself to cast away a belief that is indispensable to the rational and healthful workings of the mind? So long as the tranquil dome of heaven is raised above our heads and the firm-set earth is spread forth beneath our feet, while the everlasting stars course in their mighty orbits and the lover gazes with ineffable tenderness into the eyes of her that loves him, so long, says Faust, must our hearts go out toward Him that upholds and comprises all. Name or describe as we may the Sustainer of the world, the eternal fact remains there, far above our comprehension, yet clearest and most real of all facts. To name and describe it, to bring it within the formulas of theory or creed, is but to veil its glory

The Idea of God. 37

as when the brightness of heaven is enshrouded in mist and smoke. This has a pleasant sound to Margaret's ears. It reminds her of what the parson sometimes says, though couched in very different phrases; and yet she remains uneasy and unsatisfied. Her mind is benumbed by the presence of an idea confessedly too great to be grasped. She feels the need of some concrete symbol that can be readily apprehended; and she hopes that her lover has not been learning bad lessons from Mephistopheles.

The difficulty which here besets Margaret must doubtless have been felt by every one when confronted with the thoughts by which the highest human minds have endeavoured to disclose the hidden life of the universe and interpret its meaning. It is a difficulty which baffles many, and they who surmount it are few indeed. Most people content themselves through life with a set of concrete formulas concerning Deity, and vituperate as atheistic all conceptions which refuse to be compressed within the narrow limits of their creed. For the great mass of men the idea of God is quite overlaid and obscured by innumerable symbolic rites and doctrines that have grown up in the course of the long historic development of religion. All such rites and doctrines had a meaning once, beautiful and inspiring or terrible and forbidding, and many of them still retain it. But whether meaningless or fraught with significance, men have wildly clung to them as shipwrecked mariners cling to the drifting spars that alone give promise of rescue from threatening death. Such concrete symbols have in all ages been argued and fought for until they have come to seem the essentials of religion; and new moons and sabbaths, decrees of councils and articles of faith, have usurped the place of the living God. In every age the theory or discovery — however profoundly theistic in its real import — which has thrown discredit upon such symbols

The Idea of God.

has been stigmatized as subversive of religion, and its adherents have been reviled and persecuted. It is, of course, inevitable that this should be so. To the half-educated mind a theory of divine action couched in the form of a legend, in which God is depicted as entertaining human purposes and swayed by human passions, is not only intelligible, but impressive. It awakens emotion, it speaks to the heart, it threatens the sinner with wrath to come or heals the wounded spirit with sweet whispers of consolation. However mythical the form in which it is presented, however literally false the statements of which it is composed, it seems profoundly real and substantial. Just in so far as it is crudely concrete, just in so far as its terms can be vividly realized by the ordinary mind, does such a theological theory seem weighty and true. On the other hand, a theory of divine action which, discarding as far as possible the aid of concrete symbols, attempts to include within its range the endlessly complex operations that are forever going on throughout the length and breadth of the knowable universe,—such a theory is to the ordinary mind unintelligible. It awakens no emotion because it is not understood. Though it may be the nearest approximation to the truth of which the human intellect is at the present moment capable, though the statements of which it is composed may be firmly based upon demonstrated facts in nature, it will nevertheless seem eminently unreal and uninteresting. The dullest peasant can understand you when you tell him that honey is sweet, while a statement that the ratio of the circumference of a circle to its diameter may be expressed by the formula $\pi = 3.14159$ will sound as gibberish in his ears; yet the truth embodied in the latter statement is far more closely implicated with every act of the peasant's life, if he only knew it, than the truth expressed in the former. So the merest child may know enough to marvel at the Hebrew legend of the burning bush, but only the ripest scholar can begin to understand the character of the mighty problems with which Spinoza was grappling when he had so much to say about *natura naturans* and *natura naturata.*

For these reasons all attempts to study God as revealed in the workings of the visible universe, and to characterize the divine activity in terms derived from such study, have met with discouragement, if not with obloquy. As substituting a less easily comprehensible formula for one that is more easily comprehensible, they seem to be frittering away the idea of God, and reducing it to an empty abstraction. There is a further reason for the dread with which such studies are commonly regarded. The theories of divine action accepted as orthodox by the men of any age have been bequeathed to them by their forefathers of an earlier age. They were originally framed with reference to assumed facts of nature which advancing knowledge is continually discrediting and throwing aside. Each forward step in physical science obliges us to contemplate the universe from a somewhat altered point of view, so that the mutual relations of its parts keep changing as in an ever-shifting landscape. The notions of the world and its Maker with which we started by and by prove meagre and unsatisfying; they no longer fit in with the general scheme of our knowledge. Hence the men who are wedded to the old notions are quick to sound the alarm. They would fain deter us from taking the forward step which carries us to a new standpoint. Beware of science, they cry, lest with its dazzling discoveries and adventurous speculations it rob us of our soul's comfort and leave us in a godless world. Such in every age has been the cry of the more timid and halting spirits; and their fears have found apparent confirmation in the behaviour of a very different class of thinkers. As there are those who live in perpetual dread of the time when science shall banish God from the world, so, on the other hand, there are those who look forward with longing to such a time, and in their impatience are continually starting up and proclaiming that at last it has come. There are those who have indeed learned a lesson from Mephistopheles, the "spirit that forever denies." These are they that say in their hearts, "There is no God," and "congratulate themselves that they are going to die like the beasts." Rushing into the holiest arcana of philosophy, even where angels fear to tread, they lay hold of each new discovery in science that modifies our view of the universe, and herald it as a crowning victory for the materialists,—a victory which is ushering in the happy day when atheism is to be the creed of all men. It is in view of such philosophizers that the astronomer, the chemist, or the anatomist, whose aim is the dispassionate examination of evidence and the unbiassed study of phenomena, may fitly utter the prayer, "Lord, save me from my friends!"

Thus through age after age has it fared with men's discoveries in science, and with their thoughts about God and the soul. It was so in the days of Galileo and Newton, and we have found it to be so in the days of Darwin and Spencer. The theologian exclaims, If planets are held in place by gravitation and tangential momentum, and if the highest forms of life have been developed by natural selection and direct adaptation, then the universe is swayed by blind forces, and nothing is left for God to do: how impious and terrible the thought! Even so, echoes the favourite atheist, the Lamettrie or Büchner of the day; the universe, it seems, has always got on without a God, and accordingly there is none: how noble and cheering the thought! And as thus age after age they wrangle, with their eyes turned away from the light, the world goes on to larger and larger knowledge in spite of them, and does not lose its faith, for all these darkeners of counsel may say. As in the roaring loom of Time the endless web of events is woven, each strand shall make more and more clearly visible the living garment of God.

II.

The Rapid Growth of Modern Knowledge.

AT no time since men have dwelt upon the earth have their notions about the universe undergone so great a change as in the century of which we are now approaching the end. Never before has knowledge increased so rapidly; never before has philosophical speculation been so actively conducted, or its results so widely diffused. It is a characteristic of organic evolution that numerous progressive tendencies, for a long time inconspicuous, now and then unite to bring about a striking and apparently sudden change; or a set of forces, quietly accumulating in one direction, at length unlock some new reservoir of force and abruptly inaugurate a new series of phenomena, as when water rises in a tank until its overflow sets whirling a system of toothed wheels. It may be that Nature makes no leaps, but in this way she now and then makes very long strides. It is in this way that the course of organic development is marked here and there by memorable epochs, which seem to open new chapters in the history of the universe. There was such an epoch when the common ancestor of ascidian and amphioxus first showed rudimentary traces of a vertebral column. There was such an epoch when the air-bladder of early amphibians began to do duty as a lung. Greatest of all, since the epoch, still hidden from our ken, when organic life began upon the surface of the globe, was the birth of that new era when, through a wondrous change in the direction of the working of natural selection, Humanity appeared upon the scene. In the career of the human race we can likewise point to periods in which it has become apparent that an immense stride was taken. Such a period marks the dawning of human history, when after countless ages of desultory tribal warfare men succeeded in uniting into comparatively stable political societies, and through the medium of written language began handing down to posterity the record of their thoughts and deeds. Since that morning twilight of history there has been no era so strongly marked, no change so swift or so far-reaching in the conditions of human life, as that which began with the great maritime discoveries of the fifteenth century and is approaching its culmination to-day. In its earlier stages this modern era was signalized by sporadic achievements of the human intellect, great in themselves and leading to such stupendous results as the boldest dared not dream of. Such achievements were the invention of printing, the telescope and microscope, the geometry of Descartes, the astronomy of Newton, the physics of Huyghens, the physiology of Harvey. Man's senses were thus indefinitely enlarged as his means of registration were perfected; he became capable of extending physical inferences from the earth to the heavens; and he made his first acquaintance with that luminiferous ether which was by and by to reveal the intimate structure of matter in regions far beyond the power of the microscope to penetrate.

It is only within the present century that the vastness of the changes thus beginning to be wrought has become apparent. The scientific achievements of the human intellect no longer occur sporadically : they follow one upon another, like the organized and systematic conquests of a resistless army. Each new discovery becomes at once a powerful implement in the hands of innumerable workers, and each year wins over fresh regions of the universe from the unknown to the known. Our own generation has become so wonted to this unresting march of discovery that we already take it as quite a matter of course. Our minds become easily deadened to its real import, and the examples we cite in illustration of it have an air of triteness. We scarcely need to be reminded that all the advances made in locomotion, from the days of Nebuchadnezzar to those of Andrew Jackson, were as nothing compared to the change that has been wrought within a few years by the introduction of railroads. In these times, when Puck has fulfilled his boast and put a girdle about the earth in forty minutes, we are not yet perhaps in danger of forgetting that a century has not elapsed since he who caught the lightning upon his kite was laid in the grave. Yet the lesson of these facts, as well as of the grandmother's spinning-wheel that stands by the parlour fireside, is well to bear in mind. The change therein exemplified since Penelope plied her distaff is far less than that which has occurred within the memory of living men. The developments of machinery, which have worked such wonders, have greatly altered the political conditions of human society, so that a huge republic like the United States is now as snug and compact and easily manageable as the tiny republic of Switzerland in the eighteenth century. The number of men that can live upon a given area of the earth's surface has been multiplied manifold, and while the mass of human life has thus increased its value has been at the same time enhanced.

In these various applications of physical theory to the industrial arts, countless minds, of a class that formerly were not reached by scientific reasoning at all, are now brought into daily contact with complex and subtle operations of matter, and their habits of thought are thus notably modified. Meanwhile, in the higher regions of chemistry and molecular physics the progress has been such that no description can do it justice. When we reflect that a fourth generation has barely had time to appear on the scene since Priestley discovered that there was such a thing as oxygen, we stand awestruck before the stupendous pile of chemical science which has been reared in this brief interval. Our knowledge thus gained of the molecular and atomic structure of matter has been alone sufficient to remodel our conceptions of the universe from beginning to end. The case of molecular physics is equally striking. The theory of the conservation of energy, and the discovery that light, heat, electricity, and magnetism are differently conditioned modes of undulatory motion transformable each into the other, are not yet fifty years old. In physical astronomy we remained until 1839 confined within the limits of the solar system, and even here the Newtonian theory had not yet won its crowning triumph in the discovery of the planet Neptune. To-day we not only measure the distances and movements of many stars, but by means of spectrum analysis are able to tell what they are made of. It is more than a century since the nebular hypothesis, by which we explain the development of stellar systems, was first propounded by Immanuel Kant, but it is only within thirty years that it has been generally adopted by astronomers; and among the outward illustrations of its essential soundness none is more remarkable than its surviving such an enlargement of our knowledge. Coming to the geologic study of the changes that have taken place on the earth's surface, it was in 1830 that Sir Charles Lyell published the book which first placed this study upon a scientific basis. Cuvier's classification of past and present forms of animal life, which laid the foundations alike of comparative anatomy and of palæontology, came but little earlier. The cell-doctrine of Schleiden and Schwann, prior to which modern biology can hardly be said to have existed, dates from 1839; and it was only ten years before that the scientific treatment of embryology began with Von Baer. At the present moment, twenty-six years have not elapsed since the epoch-making work of Darwin first announced to the world the discovery of natural selection.

In the cycle of studies which are immediately concerned with the career of mankind, the rate of progress has been no less marvellous. The scientific study of human speech may be said to date from the flash of insight which led Friedrich Schlegel in 1808 to detect the kinship between the Aryan languages. From this beginning to the researches of Fick and Ascoli in our own time, the quantity of achievement rivals anything the physical sciences can show. The study of comparative mythology, which has thrown such light upon the primitive thoughts of mankind, is still younger, — is still, indeed, in its infancy. The application of the comparative method to the investigation of laws and customs, of political and ecclesiastical and industrial systems, has been carried on scarcely thirty years; yet the results already obtained are obliging us to rewrite the history of mankind in all its stages. The great achievements of archæologists — the decipherment of Egyptian hieroglyphs and of cuneiform inscriptions in Assyria and Persia, the unearthing of ancient cities, the discovery and classification of primeval implements and works of art in all quarters of the globe — belong almost entirely to the nineteenth century. These discoveries, which have well-nigh doubled for us the length of the historic period, have united with the quite modern revelations of geology concerning the ancient glaciation of the temperate zones, to give us an approximate idea of the age of the human race[1] and the circumstances attending its diffusion over the earth. It has thus at length become possible to obtain something like the outlines of a comprehensive view of the history of the creation, from the earliest stages of condensation of our solar nebula down to the very time in which we live, and to infer from the characteristics of this past evolution some of the most general tendencies of the future.

All this accumulation of physical and historical knowledge has not failed to react upon our study of the human mind itself. In books of logic the score of centuries between Aristotle and Whately saw less advance than the few years between Whately and Mill. In psychology the work of Fechner and Wundt and Spencer belongs to the age in which we are now living. When to all this variety of achievement we add what has been done in the critical study of literature and art, of classical and Biblical philology, and of metaphysics and theology, illustrating from fresh points of view the history of the human mind, the sum total becomes almost too vast to be comprehended. This century, which some have called an age of iron, has been also an age of ideas, an era of seeking and finding the like of which was never known before. It is an epoch the grandeur of which dwarfs all others that can be named since the beginning of the historic period, if not since Man first became distinctively human. In their mental habits, in their methods of inquiry, and in the data at their command, "the men of the present day who have fully kept pace with the scientific movement are separated from the men whose education ended in 1830 by an immeasurably wider gulf than has ever before divided one progressive generation of men from their predecessors."[2] The intellectual development of the human race has been suddenly, almost abruptly, raised to a higher plane than that upon which it had proceeded from the days of the primitive troglodyte to the days of our great-grandfathers. It is characteristic of this higher plane of development that the progress which until lately was so slow must henceforth be rapid. Men's minds are becoming more flexible, the resistance to innovation is weakening, and our intellectual demands are multiplying while the means of satisfying them are increasing. Vast as are the achievements we have just passed in review, the gaps in our knowledge are immense, and every problem that is solved but opens a dozen new problems that await solution. Under such circumstances there is no likelihood that the last word will soon be said on any subject. In the eyes of the twenty-first century the science of the nineteenth will doubtless seem very fragmentary and crude. But the men of that day, and of all future time, will no doubt point back to the age just passing away as the opening of a new dispensation, the dawning of an era in which the intellectual development of mankind was raised to a higher plane than that upon which it had hitherto proceeded.

As the inevitable result of the thronging discoveries just enumerated, we find ourselves in the midst of a mighty revolution in human thought. Time-honoured creeds are losing their hold upon men; ancient symbols are shorn of their value; everything is called in question. The controversies of the day are not like those of former times. It is no longer a question of hermeneutics, no longer a struggle between abstruse dogmas of rival churches. Religion itself is called upon to show why it should any longer claim our allegiance. There are those who deny the existence of God. There are those who would explain away the human soul as a mere group of fleeting phenomena attendant upon the collocation of sundry particles of matter. And there are many others who, without committing themselves to these positions of the atheist and the materialist, have nevertheless come to regard religion as practically ruled out from human affairs. No religious creed that man has ever devised can be made to harmonize in all its features with modern knowledge. All such creeds were constructed with reference to theories of the universe which are now utterly and hopelessly discredited. How, then, it is asked, amid the general wreck of old beliefs, can we hope that the religious attitude in which from time immemorial we have been wont to contemplate the universe can any longer be maintained? Is not the belief in God perhaps a dream of the childhood of our race, like the belief in elves and bogarts which once was no less universal? and is not modern science fast destroying the one as it has already destroyed the other?

Such are the questions which we daily hear asked, sometimes with flippant eagerness, but oftener with anxious dread. In view of them it is well worth while to examine the idea of God, as it has been entertained by mankind from the earliest ages, and as it is affected by the knowledge of the universe which we have acquired in recent times. If we find in that idea, as conceived by untaught thinkers in the twilight of antiquity, an element that still survives the widest and deepest generalizations of modern times, we have the strongest possible reason for believing that the idea is permanent and answers to an Eternal Reality. It was to be expected that conceptions of Deity handed down from primitive men should undergo serious modification. If it can be shown that the essential element in these conceptions must survive the enormous additions to our knowledge which have distinguished the present age above all others since man became man, then we may believe that it will endure so long as man endures; for it is not likely that it can ever be called upon to pass a severer ordeal.

All this will presently appear in a still stronger light, when we have set forth the common characteristic of the modifications which the idea of God has already undergone, and the nature of the opposition between the old and the new knowledge with which we are now confronted. Upon this discussion we have now to enter, and we shall find it leading us to the conclusion that throughout all possible advances in human knowledge, so far as we can see, the essential position of theism must remain unshaken.

III.

Sources of the Theistic Idea.

OUR argument may fitly begin with an inquiry into the sources of the theistic idea and the shape which it has universally assumed among untutored men. The most primitive element which it contains is doubtless the notion of *dependence* upon something outside of ourselves. We are born into a world consisting of forces which sway our lives and over which we can exercise no control. The individual man can indeed make his volition count for a very little in modifying the course of events, but this end necessitates strict and unceasing obedience to powers that cannot be tampered with. To the behaviour of these external powers our actions must be adapted under penalty of death. And upon grounds no less firm than those on which we believe in any externality whatever, we recognize that these forces antedated our birth and will endure after we have disappeared from the scene. No one supposes that he makes the world for himself, so that it is born and dies with him. Every one perforce contemplates the world as something existing independently of himself, as something into which he has come, and from which he is to go; and for his coming and his going, as well as for what he does while part of the world, he is dependent upon something that is not himself.

Between ancient and modern man, as between the child and the adult, there can be no essential difference in the recognition of this fundamental fact of life. The primitive man could not, indeed, state the case in this generalized form, any more than a young child could state it, but the facts which the statement covers were as real to him as they are to us.* The prim-

* See note A at the end of the volume.

itive man knew nothing of a world, in the modern sense of the word. The conception of that vast consensus of forces which we call the world or universe is a somewhat late result of culture; it was reached only through ages of experience and reflection. Such an idea lay beyond the horizon of the primitive man. But while he knew not the world, he knew bits and pieces of it; or, to vary the expression, he had his little world, chaotic and fragmentary enough, but full of dread reality for him. He knew what it was to deal from birth until death with powers far mightier than himself. To explain these powers, to make their actions in any wise intelligible, he had but one available resource; and this was so obvious that he could not fail to employ it. The only source of action of which he knew anything, since it was the only source which lay within himself, was the human will;[3] and in this respect, after all, the philosophy of the primeval savage was not so very far removed from that of the modern scientific thinker. The primitive man could see that his own actions were prompted by desire and guided by intelligence, and he supposed the same to be the case with the sun and the wind, the frost and the lightning. All the forces of outward nature, so far as they came into visible contact with his life, he personified as great beings which were to be contended with or placated. This primeval philosophy, once universal among men, has lasted far into the historic period, and it is only slowly and bit by bit that it has been outgrown by the most highly civilized races. Indeed the half-civilized majority of mankind have by no means as yet cast it aside, and among savage tribes we may still see it persisting in all its original crudity. In the mythologies of all peoples, of the Greeks and Hindus and Norsemen, as well as of the North American Indians and the dwellers in the South Sea islands, we find the sun personified as an archer or wanderer, the clouds as gigantic birds, the tempest as a devouring dragon ; and the tales of gods and heroes, as well as of trolls and fairies, are made up of scattered and distorted fragments of nature-myths, of which the primitive meaning had long been forgotten when the ingenuity of modern scholarship laid it bare.[4]

In all this personification of physical phenomena our prehistoric ancestors were greatly assisted by that theory of ghosts which was perhaps the earliest speculative effort of the human mind. Travellers have now and then reported the existence of races of men quite destitute of religion, or of what the observer has learned to recognize as religion ; but no one has ever discovered a race of men devoid of a belief in ghosts. The mass of crude inference which makes up the savage's philosophy of nature is largely based upon the hypothesis that every man has *another self*, a double, or wraith, or ghost. This "hypothesis of the *other self*, which serves to account for the savage's wanderings during sleep in strange lands and among strange people, serves also to account for the presence in his dreams of parents, comrades, or enemies, known to be dead and buried. The other self of the dreamer meets and converses with the other selves of his dead brethren, joins with them in the hunt, or sits down with them to the wild cannibal banquet. Thus arises the belief in an ever-present world of ghosts, a belief which the entire experience of uncivilized man goes to strengthen and expand."[5] Countless tales and superstitions of savage races show that the hypothesis of the other self is used to explain the phenomena of hysteria and epilepsy, of shadows, of echoes, and even of the reflection of face and gestures in still water. It is not only men, moreover, who are provided with other selves. Dumb beasts and plants, stone hatchets and arrows, articles of clothing and food, all have their ghosts;[6] and when the dead chief is buried, his wives and servants, his dogs and horses, are slain to keep him company, and weapons and trinkets are placed in his tomb to be used in the spirit-land. Burial-places of primitive men, ages before the dawn of history, bear testimony to the immense antiquity of this savage philosophy. From this wholesale belief in ghosts to the interpretation of the wind or the lightning as a person animated by an indwelling soul and endowed with quasi-human passions and purposes, the step is not a long one. The latter notion grows almost inevitably out of the former, so that all races of men without exception have entertained it. That the mighty power which uproots trees and drives the storm-clouds across the sky should resemble a human soul is to the savage an unavoidable inference. "If the fire burns down his hut, it is because the fire is a person with a soul, and is angry with him, and needs to be coaxed into a kindlier mood by means of prayer or sacrifice." He has no alternative but to regard fire-soul as something akin to human-soul; his philosophy makes no distinction between the human ghost and the elemental demon or deity.

It was in accordance with this primitive theory of things that the earliest form of religious worship was developed. In all races of men, so far as can be determined, this was the worship of ancestors.[7] The other self of the dead chieftain continued after death to watch over the interests of the tribe, to defend it against the attacks of enemies, to reward brave warriors, and to punish traitors and cowards. His favour must be propitiated with ceremonies like those in which a subject does homage to a living ruler. If offended by neglect or irreverent treatment, defeat in battle, damage by flood or fire, visitations of famine or pestilence, were interpreted as marks of his anger. Thus the spirits animating the forces of nature were often identified with the ghosts of ancestors, and mythology is filled with traces of the confusion. In the Vedic religion the *pitris*, or "fathers," live in the sky along with Yama, the original *pitri* of mankind: they are very busy with the weather; they send down rain to refresh the thirsty earth, or anon parch the fields till the crops perish of drought; and they rush along in the roaring tempest, like the weird host of the wild huntsman Wodan. To the ancient Greek the blue sky Uranos was the father of gods and men, and throughout antiquity this mingling of ancestor-worship with nature-worship was general. With the systematic development of ethnic religions, in some instances ancestor-worship remained dominant, as with the Chinese, the Japanese, and the Romans; in others, a polytheism based upon nature-worship acquired supremacy, as with the Hindus and Greeks, and our own Teutonic forefathers. The great divinities of the Hellenic pantheon are all personifications of physical phenomena. At a comparatively late date the Roman adopted these divinities and paid to them a fashionable and literary homage, but his solemn and heartfelt rites were those with which he worshipped the *lares* and *penates* in the privacy of his home. His hospitable treatment of the gods of a vanquished people was the symptom of a commingling of the various local religions of antiquity which insured their mutual destruction and prepared the way for their absorption into a far grander and truer system.[8]

IV.

Development of Monotheism.

SUCH an allusion to the Romans, in an exposition like the present one, is not without its significance. It was partly through political circumstances that a truly theistic idea was developed out of the chaotic and fragmentary ghost theories and nature-worship of the primeval world. To the framing of the vastest of all possible conceptions, the idea of God, man came but slowly. This nature-worship and ancestor-worship of early times was scarcely theism. In their recognition of man's utter dependence upon something outside of himself which yet was not wholly unlike himself, these primitive religions contained the essential germ out of which theism was to grow; but it is a long way from the propitiation of ghosts and the adoration of the rising sun to the worship of the infinite and eternal God, the maker of heaven and earth, in whom we live, and move, and have our being. Before men could arrive at such a conception, it was necessary for them to obtain some integral idea of the heaven and the earth; it was necessary for them to frame, however inadequately, the conception of a physical universe. Such a conception had been reached by civilized peoples before the Christian era, and by the Greeks a remarkable beginning had been made in the generalization and interpretation of physical phenomena. The intellectual atmosphere of Alexandria, for two centuries before and three centuries after the time of Christ, was more modern than anything that followed down to the days of Bacon and Descartes; and all the leaders of Greek thought since Anaxagoras had been virtually or avowedly monotheists. As the phenomena of nature were generalized, the deities or superhuman beings regarded as their sources were likewise generalized, until the conception of nature as a whole gave rise to the conception of a single Deity as the author and ruler of nature; and in accordance with the order of its genesis, this notion of Deity was still the notion of a Being possessed of psychical attributes, and in some way like unto Man.

But there was another cause, besides scientific generalization, which led men's minds toward monotheism. The conception of tutelar deities, which was the most prominent practical feature of ancestor-worship, was directly affected by the political development of the peoples of antiquity. As tribes were consolidated into nations, the tutelar gods of the tribes became generalized, or the god of some leading tribe came to supersede his fellows, until the result was a single national deity, at first regarded as the greatest among gods, afterwards as the only God. The most striking instance of this method of

The Idea of God. 75

development is afforded by the Hebrew
conception of Jehovah. The most primitive form of Hebrew religion discernible
in the Old Testament is a fetichism, or
very crude polytheism, in which ancestor-worship becomes more prominent than
nature-worship. At first the *teraphim*, or
tutelar household deities, play an important part, but nature-gods, such as Baal,
and Moloch, and Astarte, are extensively
worshipped. It is the plural *elohim* who
create the earth, and whose sons visit the
daughters of antediluvian men. The tutelar deity, Jehovah, is originally thought of
as one of the *elohim*, then as chief among
elohim, and Lord of the hosts of heaven.
Through his favour his chosen prophet
overcomes the prophets of Baal, he is
greater than the deities of neighbouring
peoples, he is the only true god, and thus
finally he is thought of as the only God,
and his name becomes the symbol of monotheism. The Jews have always been one
of the most highly-gifted races in the

world. In antiquity they developed an intense sentiment of nationality, and for earnestness and depth of ethical feeling they surpassed all other peoples. The conception of Jehovah set forth in the writings of the prophets was the loftiest conception of deity anywhere attained before the time of Christ; in ethical value it immeasurably surpassed anything to be found in the pantheon of the Greeks and Romans. It was natural that such a conception of deity should be adopted throughout the Roman world. At the beginning of the Christian era the classic polytheism had well-nigh lost its hold upon men's minds; its value had become chiefly literary, as a mere collection of pretty stories; it had begun its descent into the humble realm of folk-lore. For want of anything better people had recourse to elaborate Eastern ceremonials, or contented themselves with the time-honoured domestic worship of the *lares* and *penates*. Yet their minds were ripe for some kind of monotheism, and in order that the Jewish conception should come to be generally adopted, it was only necessary that it should be freed from its limitations of nationality, and that Jehovah should be set forth as Sustainer of the universe and Father of all mankind. This was done by Jesus and Paul. The theory of divine action implied throughout the gospels and the epistles was the first complete monotheism attained by mankind, or at least by that portion of it from which our modern civilization has descended. Here for the first time we have the idea of God dissociated from the limiting circumstances with which it had been entangled in all the ethnic religions of antiquity. Individual thinkers here and there had already, doubtless, reached an equally true conception, as was shown by Kleanthes in his sublime hymn to Zeus;[9] but it was now for the first time set forth in such wise as to win assent from the common folk as well as the philosophers, and to make its way into the hearts of all men. Its acceptance was hastened, and its hold upon mankind immeasurably strengthened, by the divinely beautiful ethical teaching in which Jesus couched it, — that teaching, so often misunderstood yet so profoundly true, which heralded the time when Man shall have thrown off the burden of his bestial inheritance and strife and sorrow shall cease from the earth.[10]

We shall presently see that in its fundamental features the theism of Jesus and Paul was so true that it must endure as long as man endures. Changes of statement may alter the outward appearance of it, but the kernel of truth will remain the same forever. But the shifting body of religious doctrine known as Christianity has at various times contained much that is unknown to this pure theism, and much that has shown itself to be ephemeral in its hold upon men. The change from polytheism to monotheism could not be thoroughly accomplished all at once. As

Christianity spread over the Roman world it became encrusted with pagan notions and observances, and a similar process went on during the conversion of the Teutonic barbarians. Yuletide and Easter and other church holidays were directly adopted from the old nature-worship; the adoration of tutelar household deities survived in the homage paid to patron saints; and the worship of the Berecynthian Mother was continued in that of the Virgin Mary.[11] Even the name *God*, applied to the Deity throughout Teutonic Christendom, seems to be neither more nor less than *Wodan*, the personification of the storm-wind, the supreme divinity of our pagan forefathers.*

That Christianity should thus have retained names and symbols and rites belonging to heathen antiquity was inevitable. The system of Christian theism was the work of some of the loftiest minds that have ever appeared upon the earth; but it was adopted by millions of men and women, of

* See note B. at the end of the volume.

all degrees of knowledge and ignorance, of keenness and dullness, of spirituality and grossness, and these brought to it their various inherited notions and habits of thought. In all its ages, therefore, Christian theism has meant one thing to one person, and another thing to another. While the highest Christian minds have always been monotheistic, the multitude have outgrown polytheism but slowly; and even the monotheism of the highest minds has been coloured by notions ultimately derived from the primeval ghost-world which have interfered with its purity, and have seriously hampered men in their search after truth.

In illustration of this point we have now to notice two strongly contrasted views of the divine nature which have been held by Christian theists, and to observe their bearings upon the scientific thought of modern times.

V.

The Idea of God as immanent in the World.

WE have seen that since the primitive savage philosophy did not distinguish between the human ghost and the elemental demon or deity, the religion of antiquity was an inextricable tangle of ancestor-worship with nature-worship. Nevertheless, among some peoples the one, among others the other, became predominant. I think it can hardly be an accidental coincidence that nature-worship predominated with the Greeks and Hindus, the only peoples of antiquity who accomplished anything in the exact sciences, or in metaphysics. The capacity for abstract thinking which led the Hindu to originate algebra, and the Greek to originate geometry, and both to attempt elaborate scientific theories of the universe, —

this same capacity revealed itself in the manner in which they deified the powers of nature. They were able to imagine the indwelling spirit of the sun or the storm without help from the conception of an individual ghost. Such being the general capacity of the people, we can readily understand how, when it came to monotheism, their most eminent thinkers should have been able to frame the conception of God acting in and through the powers of nature, without the aid of any grossly anthropomorphic symbolism. In this connection it is interesting to observe the characteristics of the idea of God as conceived by the three greatest fathers of the Greek church, Clement of Alexandria, Origen, and Athanasius. The philosophy of these profound and vigorous thinkers was in large measure derived from the Stoics. They regarded Deity as immanent in the universe, and eternally operating through natural laws. In their view God is not a localizable personality, remote from the world, and acting upon it only by means of occasional portent and prodigy; nor is the world a lifeless machine blindly working after some preordained method, and only feeling the presence of God in so far as he now and then sees fit to interfere with its normal course of procedure. On the contrary, God is the ever-present life of the world; it is through him that all things exist from moment to moment, and the natural sequence of events is a perpetual revelation of the divine wisdom and goodness. In accordance with this fundamental view, Clement, for example, repudiated the Gnostic theory of the vileness of matter, condemned asceticism, and regarded the world as hallowed by the presence of indwelling Deity. Knowing no distinction "between what man discovers and what God reveals," he explained Christianity as a natural development from the earlier religious thought of mankind. It was essential to his idea of the divine perfection that the past should contain within itself all the germs of the future;

and accordingly he attached but slight value to tales of miracle, and looked upon salvation as the normal ripening of the higher spiritual qualities of man "under the guidance of immanent Deity." The views of Clement's disciple Origen are much like those of his master. Athanasius ventured much farther into the bewildering regions of metaphysics. Yet in his doctrine of the Trinity, by which he overcame the visible tendency toward polytheism in the theories of Arius, and averted the threatened danger of a compromise between Christianity and Paganism, he proceeded upon the lines which Clement had marked out. In his very suggestive work on "The Continuity of Christian Thought," Professor Alexander Allen thus sets forth the Athanasian point of view: "In the formula of Father, Son, and Holy Spirit, as three distinct and co-equal members in the one divine essence, there was the recognition and the reconciliation of the philosophical schools which had divided the ancient world. In the idea of the eternal Father the Oriental mind recognized what it liked to call the profound abyss of being, that which lies back of all phenomena, the hidden mystery which lends awe to human minds seeking to know the divine. In the doctrine of the eternal Son revealing the Father, immanent in nature and humanity as the life and light shining through all created things, the divine reason in which the human reason shares, there was the recognition of the truth after which Plato and Aristotle and the Stoics were struggling, — the tie which binds the creation to God in the closest organic relationship. In the doctrine of the Holy Spirit the church guarded against any pantheistic confusion of God with the world by upholding the life of the manifested Deity as essentially ethical or spiritual, revealing itself in humanity in its highest form, only in so far as humanity recognized its calling and through the Spirit entered into communion with the Father and the Son."

Great as was the service which these

views of Athanasius rendered in the fourth century of our era, they are scarcely to be regarded as a permanent or essential feature of Christian theism. The metaphysic in which they are couched is alien to the metaphysic of our time, yet through this vast difference it is all the more instructive to note how closely Athanasius approaches the confines of modern scientific thought, simply through his fundamental conception of God as the indwelling life of the universe. We shall be still more forcibly struck with this similarity when we come to consider the character impressed upon our idea of God by the modern doctrine of evolution.

VI.

The Idea of God as remote from the World.

BUT this Greek conception of divine immanence did not find favour with the Latin-speaking world. There a very different notion prevailed, the origin of which may be traced to the mental habits attending the primitive ancestor-worship. Out of materials furnished by the ghost-world a crude kind of monotheism could be reached by simply carrying back the thought to a single ghost-deity as the original ancestor of all the others. Some barbarous races have gone as far as this, as for example the Zulus, who have developed the doctrine of divine ancestors so far as to recognize a first ancestor, the Great Father, Unkulunkulu, who created the world.[12] The kind of theism reached by this process of thought differs essentially from the theism reached through the medium of nature-worship. For whereas in the latter case the god of the sky or the sea is regarded as a mysterious spirit acting in and through the phenomena, in the former case the phenomena are regarded as coerced into activity by some power existing outside of them, and this power is conceived as manlike in the crudest sense, having been originally thought of as the ghost of some man who once lived upon the earth. In the monotheism which is reached by thinking along these lines of inference, the universe is conceived as an inert lifeless machine, impelled by blind forces which have been set acting from without; and God is conceived as existing apart from the world in solitary inaccessible majesty, — "an absentee God," as Carlyle says, "sitting idle ever since the first Sabbath, at the outside of his universe, and 'seeing it go.'" This conception demands less of the intellect than the conception of God as immanent in the universe. It requires less grasp of mind and less width of experience, and it has accordingly been much the more common conception. The idea of the indwelling God is an attempt to reach out toward the reality, and as such it taxes the powers of the finite mind. The idea of God external to the universe is a symbol which in no wise approaches the reality, and for that very reason it does not tax the mental powers; there is an aspect of finality about it, in which the ordinary mind rests content and complains of whatever seeks to disturb its repose.

I must not be understood as ignoring the fact that this lower species of theism has been entertained by some of the loftiest minds of our race, both in ancient and in modern times. When once such an ever-present conception as the idea of God has become intertwined with the whole body of the thoughts of mankind, it is very difficult for the most powerful and subtle intelligence to change the form it has taken. It has become so far organized into the texture of the mind that it abides there unconsciously, like our fundamental axioms about number and magnitude; it sways our thought hither and thither without our knowing it. The two forms of theism here contrasted have slowly grown up under the myriad unassignable influences that in antiquity caused nature-worship to predominate among some people and ancestor-worship among others; they have coloured all the philosophizing that has been done for more than twenty centuries; and it is seldom that a thinker educated under the one form ever comes to adopt the other and habitually employ it, save under the mighty influence of modern science, the tendency of which, as we shall presently see, is all in one direction.

Among ancient thinkers the view of Deity as remote from the world prevailed with the followers of Epikuros, who held that the immortal gods could not be sup-

The Idea of God.

posed to trouble themselves about the paltry affairs of men, but lived a blessed life of their own, undisturbed in the far-off empyrean. This left the world quite under the sway of blind forces, and thus we find it depicted in the marvellous poem of Lucretius, one of the loftiest monuments of Latin genius. It is to all appearance an atheistic world, albeit the author was perhaps more profoundly religious in spirit than any other Roman that ever lived, save Augustine; yet to his immediate scientific purpose this atheism was no drawback. When we are investigating natural phenomena, with intent to explain them scientifically, our proper task is simply to ascertain the physical conditions under which they occur, and the less we meddle with metaphysics or theology the better. As Laplace said, the mathematician, in solving his equations, does not need "the hypothesis of God."[13] To the scientific investigator, as such, the forces of nature are doubtless blind, like the x

and *y* in algebra, but this is only so long as he contents himself with describing their modes of operation ; when he undertakes to explain them philosophically, as we shall see, he can in no wise dispense with his theistic hypothesis. The Lucretian philosophy, therefore, admirable as a scientific coördination of such facts about the physical universe as were then known, goes but very little way as a philosophy. It is interesting to note that this atheism followed directly from that species of theism which placed God outside of his universe. We shall find the case of modern atheism to be quite similar. As soon as this crude and misleading conception of God is refuted, as the whole progress of scientific knowledge tends to refute it, the modern atheist or positivist falls back upon his universe of blind forces and contents himself with it, while zealously shouting from the housetops that this is the whole story.

To one familiar with Christian ideas, the

notion that Man is too insignificant a creature to be worth the notice of Deity seems at once pathetic and grotesque. In the view of Plato, by which all Christendom has been powerfully influenced, there is profound pathos. The wickedness and misery of the world wrought so strongly upon Plato's keen sympathies and delicate moral sense that he came to conclusions almost as gloomy as those of the Buddhist who regards existence as an evil. In the Timaios he depicts the material world as essentially vile; he is unable to think of the pure and holy Deity as manifested in it, and he accordingly separates the Creator from his creation by the whole breadth of infinitude. This view passed on to the Gnostics, for whom the puzzling problem of philosophy was how to explain the action of the spiritual God upon the material universe. Sometimes the interval was bridged by mediating æons or emanations partly spiritual and partly material; sometimes the world was held to be the work of the devil, and in no sense divine.[14] The Greek fathers under the lead of Clement, espousing the higher theism, kept clear of this torrent of Gnostic thought; but upon Augustine it fell with full force, and he was carried away with it. In his earlier writings Augustine showed himself not incapable of comprehending the views of Clement and Athanasius; but his intense feeling of man's wickedness dragged him irresistibly in the opposite direction. In his doctrine of original sin, he represents humanity as cut off from all relationship with God, who is depicted as a crudely anthropomorphic Being far removed from the universe and accessible only through the mediating offices of an organized church. Compared with the thoughts of the Greek fathers this was a barbaric conception, but it was suited alike to the lower grade of culture in western Europe, and to the Latin political genius, which in the decline of the Empire was already occupying itself with its great and beneficent work of constructing an imperial Church. For these reasons the Augustinian theology prevailed, and in the Dark Ages which followed it became so deeply inwrought into the innermost fibres of Latin Christianity that it remains dominant to-day alike in Catholic and Protestant churches. With few exceptions every child born of Christian parents in western Europe or in America grows up with an idea of God the outlines of which were engraven upon men's minds by Augustine fifteen centuries ago. Nay, more, it is hardly too much to say that three fourths of the body of doctrine currently known as Christianity, unwarranted by Scripture and never dreamed of by Christ or his apostles, first took coherent shape in the writings of this mighty Roman, who was separated from the apostolic age by an interval of time like that which separates us from the invention of printing and the discovery of America. The idea of God upon which all this Augustinian doctrine is based is the idea of a Being actuated by human passions and purposes, localizable in space and utterly remote from that inert machine, the universe in which we live, and upon which He acts intermittently through the suspension of what are called natural laws. So deeply has this conception penetrated the thought of Christendom that we continually find it at the bottom of the speculations and arguments of men who would warmly repudiate it as thus stated in its naked outlines. It dominates the reasonings alike of believers and skeptics, of theists and atheists; it underlies at once the objections raised by orthodoxy against each new step in science and the assaults made by materialism upon every religious conception of the world; and thus it is chiefly responsible for that complicated misunderstanding which, by a lamentable confusion of thought, is commonly called "the conflict between religion and science."

VII.

Conflict between the Two Ideas, commonly misunderstood as a Conflict between Religion and Science.

IN illustration of the mischief that has been wrought by the Augustinian conception of Deity, we may cite the theological objections urged against the Newtonian theory of gravitation and the Darwinian theory of natural selection. Leibnitz, who as a mathematician but little inferior to Newton himself might have been expected to be easily convinced of the truth of the theory of gravitation, was nevertheless deterred by theological scruples from accepting it. It appeared to him that it substituted the action of physical forces for the direct action of the Deity. Now the fallacy of this argument of Leibnitz is easy to detect. It lies in a metaphysical misconception of the meaning of the word "force." "Force" is implicitly regarded as a sort of entity or dæmon which has a mode of action distinguishable from that of Deity; otherwise it is meaningless to speak of substituting the one for the other. But such a personification of "force" is a remnant of barbaric thought, in no wise sanctioned by physical science. When astronomy speaks of two planets as attracting each other with a "force" which varies directly as their masses and inversely as the squares of their distances apart, it simply uses the phrase as a convenient metaphor by which to describe the manner in which the observed movements of the two bodies occur. It explains that in presence of each other the two bodies are observed to change their positions in a certain specified way, and this is all that it means. This is all that a strictly scientific hypothesis can possibly allege, and this is all that observation can possibly prove. Whatever goes beyond this and imagines or asserts a kind of "pull" between the two bodies, is not science, but metaphysics. An atheistic metaphysics may imagine such a "pull," and may interpret it as the action of something that is not Deity, but such a conclusion can find no support in the scientific theorem, which is simply a generalized description of phenomena. The general considerations upon which the belief in the existence and direct action of Deity is otherwise founded are in no wise disturbed by the establishment of any such scientific theorem. We are still perfectly free to maintain that it is the direct action of Deity which is manifested in the planetary movements; having done nothing more with our Newtonian hypothesis than to construct a happy formula for expressing the mode or order of the manifestation. We may have learned something new concerning the manner of divine action; we certainly have not "substituted" any other kind of action for it. And what is thus obvious in this simple astronomical example is equally true in principle in every case whatever in which one set of phenomena is interpreted by reference to another set. In no case whatever can science use the words "force" or "cause" except as metaphorically descriptive of some observed or observable sequence of phenomena. And consequently at no imaginable future time, so long as the essential conditions of human thinking are maintained, can science even attempt to substitute the action of any other power for the direct action of Deity. The theological objection urged by Leibnitz against Newton was repeated word for word by Agassiz in his comments upon Darwin. He regarded it as a fatal objection to the Darwinian theory that it appeared to substitute the action of physical forces for the creative action of Deity. The fallacy here is precisely the same as in Leibnitz's argument. Mr. Darwin has convinced us that the existence of highly complicated organisms is the result of an infinitely diversified aggregate of circumstances so minute as severally to seem trivial or accidental; yet the consistent theist will always occupy an impregnable position in maintaining that the entire series in each and every one of its incidents is an immediate manifestation of the creative action of God.

In this connection it is worth while to state explicitly what is the true province of scientific explanation. Is it not obvious that since a philosophical theism must regard divine power as the immediate source of all phenomena alike, therefore science cannot properly explain any particular group of phenomena by a direct reference to the action of Deity? Such a reference is not an explanation, since it adds nothing to our previous knowledge either of the phenomena or of the manner of divine action. The business of science is simply to ascertain in what manner phenomena coexist with each other or follow each other, and the only kind of explanation with which it can properly deal is that which refers one set of phenomena to another set. In pursuing this, its legitimate business, science does not touch on the province of theology in any way, and there is no conceivable occasion for any conflict between the two. From this and the previous considerations taken together it follows not only that such explanations as are contained in the Newtonian and Darwinian theories are entirely consistent with theism, but also that they are the only kind of explanations with which science can properly concern itself at all. To say that complex organisms were directly created by the Deity is to make an assertion which, however true in a theistic sense, is utterly barren. It is of no profit to theism, which must be taken for granted before the assertion can be made; and it is of no profit to science, which must still ask its question, "How?" [15]

We are now prepared to see that the theological objection urged against the Newtonian and Darwinian theories has its roots in that imperfect kind of theism which Augustine did so much to fasten upon the western world. Obviously if Leibnitz and Agassiz had been educated in that higher theism shared by Clement and Athanasius in ancient times with Spinoza and Goethe in later days, — if they had been accustomed to conceive of God as immanent in the universe and eternally creative, — then the argument which they urged with so much feeling would never have occurred to them. By no possibility could such an argument have entered their minds. To conceive of "physical forces" as powers of which the action could in any wise be "substituted" for the action of Deity would in such case have been absolutely impossible. Such a conception involves the idea of God as remote from the world and acting upon it from outside. The whole notion of what theological writers are fond of calling "secondary causes" involves such an idea of God. The higher or Athanasian theism knows nothing of secondary causes in a world where every event flows directly from the eternal First Cause. It knows nothing of physical forces save as immediate manifestations of the omnipresent creative power of God. In the personification of physical forces, and the implied contrast between their action and that of Deity, there is something very like a survival of the habits of thought which characterized ancient polytheism. What are these personified forces but little gods who are supposed to be invading the sacred domain of the ruler Zeus? When one speaks of substituting the action of Gravitation for the direct action of Deity, does there not hover somewhere in the dim background of the conception a vague spectre of Gravitation in the guise of a rebellious Titan? Doubtless it would not be easy to bring any one to acknowledge such a charge, but the unseen and unacknowledged part of a fallacy is just that which is most persistent and mischievous. It is not so many generations, after all, since our ancestors were barbarians and polytheists; and fragments of their barbaric thinking are continually intruding unawares into the midst of our lately-acquired scientific culture. In most philosophical discussions a great deal of loose phraseology is used, in order to find the proper connotations of which we must go back to primitive and untutored ages. Such is eminently the case with the phrases in which the forces of nature are personified and described as something else than manifestations of omnipresent Deity.

This subject is of such immense importance that I must illustrate it from yet another point of view. We must observe the manner in which, along with the progress of scientific discovery, theological arguments have come to be permeated by the strange assumption that the greater part of the universe is godless. Here again we must go back for a moment to the primeval world and observe how behind every physical phenomenon there were supposed to be quasi-human passions and a quasi-human will. Now the phenomena which were first arranged and systematized in men's thoughts, and thus made the subject of something like scientific generalization, were the simplest, the most accessible, and the most manageable phenomena; and from these the conception of a quasi-human will soonest faded away. There are savages who believe that hatchets and kettles have souls, but men unquestionably outgrew such a belief as this long before they outgrew the belief that there are ghost-like deities in the tempest, or in the sun and moon. After many ages of culture, men ceased to regard the familiar and regularly-recurring phenomena of nature as immediate results of volition, and reserved this primeval explanation for unusual or terrible phenomena, such as comets and eclipses, or famines and plagues. As the result of these habits of thought, in course of time, Nature seemed to be divided into two antithetical provinces. On the one hand, there were the phenomena that occurred with a simple regularity which seemed to exclude the idea of capricious volition; and these were supposed to constitute the realm of natural law. On the other hand, there were the complex and irregular phenomena in which the presence of law could not so easily be detected; and these were supposed to constitute the realm of immediate divine action. This antithesis has forever haunted the minds of men imbued with the lower or Augustinian theism; and such have made up the larger part of the Christian world. It has tended to make the theologians hostile to science and the men of science hostile to theology. For as scientific generalization has steadily extended the region of natural law, the region which theology has assigned to divine action has steadily diminished. Every discovery in science has stripped off territory from the latter province and added it to the former. Every such discovery has accordingly been promulgated and established in the teeth of bitter and violent opposition on the part of theologians. A desperate fight it has been for some centuries, in which science has won every disputed position, while theology, untaught by perennial defeat, still valiantly defends the little corner that is left it. Still as of old the ordinary theologian rests his case upon the assumption of disorder, caprice, and miraculous interference with the course of nature. He naively asks, "If plants and animals have been naturally originated, if the world as a whole has been evolved and not manufactured, and if human actions conform to law, what is there left for God to do? If not formally repudiated, is he not thrust back into the past eternity, as an ultimate source of things, which is postulated for form's sake, but might as well, for all practical purposes, be omitted?" [16]

The scientific inquirer may reply that the difficulty is one which theology has created for itself. It is certainly not science that has relegated the creative activ ity of God to some nameless moment in the bygone eternity and left him without occupation in the present world. It is not science that is responsible for the mischievous distinction between divine action and natural law. That distinction is historically derived from a loose habit of philosophizing characteristic of ignorant ages, and was bequeathed to modern times by the theology of the Latin church. Small blame to the atheist who, starting upon such a basis, thinks he can interpret the universe without the idea of God! He is but doing as well as he knows how, with the materials given him. One has only, however, to adopt the higher theism of Clement and Athanasius, and this alleged antagonism between science and theology, by which so many hearts have been saddened, so many minds darkened, vanishes at once and forever. "Once really adopt the conception of an ever-present God, without whom not a sparrow falls to the ground, and it becomes self-evident that the law of gravitation is but an expression of a particular mode of divine action. And what is thus true of one law is true of all laws."[17] The thinker in whose mind divine action is thus identified with orderly action, and to whom a really irregular phenomenon would seem like a manifestation of sheer diabolism, foresees in every possible extension of knowledge a fresh confirmation of his faith in God. From his point of view there can be no antagonism between our duty as inquirers and our duty as worshippers. To him no part of the universe is godless. In the swaying to and fro of molecules and the ceaseless pulsations of ether, in the secular shiftings of planetary orbits, in the busy work of frost and raindrop, in the mysterious sprouting of the seed, in the everlasting tale of death and life renewed, in the dawning of the babe's intelligence, in the varied deeds of men from age to age, he finds that which awakens the soul to reverential awe; and each act of scientific explanation but reveals an opening through which shines the glory of the Eternal Majesty.

VIII.

Anthropomorphic Conceptions of God.

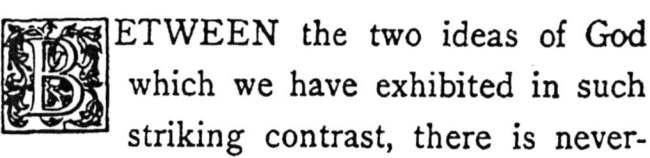

BETWEEN the two ideas of God which we have exhibited in such striking contrast, there is nevertheless one point of resemblance; and this point is fundamental, since it is the point in virtue of which both are entitled to be called theistic ideas. In both there is presumed to be a likeness of some sort between God and Man. In both there is an element of anthropomorphism. Even upon this their common ground, however, there is a wide difference between the two conceptions. In the one the anthropomorphic element is gross, in the other it is refined and subtle. The difference is so far-reaching that some years ago I proposed to mark it by contrasting these two conceptions of God as Anthropomorphic

Theism and Cosmic Theism. For the doctrine which represents God as immanent in the universe and revealing himself in the orderly succession of events, the name Cosmic Theism is eminently appropriate: but it is not intended by the antithetic nomenclature to convey the impression that in cosmic theism there is nothing anthropomorphic.[18] A theory which should regard the Human Soul as alien and isolated in the universe, without any links uniting it with the eternal source of existence, would not be theism at all. It would be Atheism, which on its metaphysical side is "the denial of anything psychical in the universe outside of human consciousness." It is far enough from any such doctrine to the cosmic theism of Clement and Origen, of Spinoza and Lessing and Schleiermacher. The difference, however, between this cosmic conception of God and the anthropomorphic conception held by Tertullian and Augustine, Calvin and Voltaire and Paley,

The Idea of God.

is sufficiently great to be described as a contrast. The explanation of the difference must be sought far back in the historic genesis of the two conceptions. Cosmic theism, as we have seen, was reached through nature-worship with its notion of vast elemental spirits indwelling in physical phenomena. Anthropomorphic theism is descended from the notion of tutelar deities which was part of the primitive ancestor-worship. In the process by which men attained to cosmic theism, physical generalization was the chief agency at work; but into anthropomorphic theism, as we have seen, there entered conceptions derived from men's political thinking. For such a people as the Romans, who could deify Imperator Augustus in just the same way that the Japanese have deified their Mikado, it was natural and easy to conceive of God as a monarch enthroned in the heavens and surrounded by a court of ministering angels. Such was the popular conception in the early ages of Christianity, and such it has doubtless remained with the mass of uninstructed people even to this day. The very grotesqueness of the idea, as it appears to the mind of a philosopher, is an index of the ease with which it satisfies the mind of an uneducated man. Many persons, no doubt, have entertained this idea of God without ever giving it very definite shape, and many have recognized it as in great measure symbolic: yet nothing can be more certain than that untold thousands have conceived it in its full intensity of anthropomorphism. Alike in sermons and theological treatises, in stately poetry and in every-day talk, the Deity has been depicted as pleased or angry, as repenting of his own acts, as soothed by adulation and quick to wreak vengeance upon silly people for blasphemous remarks. In those curious bills of expenses for the mediæval miracle-plays, along with charges of twopence for keeping up a "fyre at hell mouthe," we find such items as a shilling for a purple coat for God. In one of these plays an angel who has just witnessed the crucifixion comes rushing into Heaven, crying, "Wake up, almighty Father! Here are those beggarly Jews killing your son, and you asleep here like a drunkard!" "Devil take me if I knew anything about it!" is the drowsy reply. Not the slightest irreverence was intended in these miracle-plays, which were the only dramatic performances tolerated by the mediæval church, for the sake of their wholesome educational influence upon the common people. In the light of such facts, one sees that the representations of the Deity as an old man of august presence, with flowing hair and beard, by the early modern painters, must have meant to all save the highest minds much more than a mere symbol. Until one's thoughts have become accustomed to range far and wide over the universe it is doubtless impossible to frame a conception of Deity that is not grossly anthropomorphic. I remember distinctly the conception which I had formed when five years of age. I imagined a narrow office just over the zenith, with a tall standing-desk running lengthwise, upon which lay several open ledgers bound in coarse leather. There was no roof over this office, and the walls rose scarcely five feet from the floor, so that a person standing at the desk could look out upon the whole world. There were two persons at the desk, and one of them — a tall, slender man, of aquiline features, wearing spectacles, with a pen in his hand and another behind his ear — was God. The other, whose appearance I do not distinctly recall, was an attendant angel. Both were diligently watching the deeds of men and recording them in the ledgers. To my infant mind this picture was not grotesque, but ineffably solemn, and the fact that all my words and acts were thus written down, to confront me at the day of judgment, seemed naturally a matter of grave concern.

The Idea of God.

If we could cross-question all the men and women we know, and still more all the children, we should probably find that, even in this enlightened age, the conceptions of Deity current throughout the civilized world contain much that is in the crudest sense anthropomorphic. Such, at any rate, seems to be the character of the conceptions with which we start in life. With those whose studies lead them to ponder upon the subject in the light of enlarged experience, these conceptions become greatly modified. They lose their anthropomorphic definiteness, they grow vague by reason of their expansion, they become recognized as largely symbolic, but they never quite lose all traces of their primitive form. Indeed, as I said a moment ago, they cannot do so. The utter demolition of anthropomorphism would be the demolition of theism. We have now to see what traces of its primitive form the idea of God can retain, in the light of our modern knowledge of the universe.

IX.

The Argument from Design.

THE most highly refined and scientific form of anthropomorphic theism is that which we are accustomed to associate with Paley and the authors of the Bridgewater treatises. It is not peculiar to Christianity, since it has been held by pagans and unbelievers as firmly as by the devoutest members of the church. The argument from design is as old as Sokrates, and was relied on by Voltaire and the English deists of the eighteenth century no less than by Dr. Chalmers and Sir Charles Bell. Upon this theory the universe is supposed to have been created by a Being possessed of intelligence and volition essentially similar to the intelligence and volition of Man. This Being is actuated by a desire for the good of his creatures, and in pursuance thereof entertains purposes and adapts means to ends with consummate ingenuity. The process by which the world was created was analogous to manufacture, as being the work of an intelligent artist operating upon unintelligent materials objectively existing. It is in accordance with this theory that books on natural theology, as well as those text-books of science which deem it edifying to introduce theological reflections where they have no proper place, are fond of speaking of the "Divine Architect" or the "Great Designer."

This theory, which is still commonly held, was in high favour during the earlier part of the present century. In view of the great and sudden advances which physical knowledge was making, it seemed well worth while to consecrate science to the service of theology; and at the same time, in emphasizing the argument from design, theology adopted the methods of science. The attempt to discover evidences of beneficent purpose in the structure of the eye and ear, in the distribution of plants and animals over the earth's surface, in the shapes of the planetary orbits and the inclinations of their axes, or in any other of the innumerable arrangements of nature, was an attempt at true induction; and high praise is due to the able men who have devoted their energies to reinforcing the argument. By far the greater part of the evidence was naturally drawn from the organic world, which began to be comprehensively studied in the mutual relations of all its parts in the time of Lamarck and Cuvier. The organic world is full of unspeakably beautiful and wonderful adaptations between organisms and their environments, as well as between the various parts of the same organism. The unmistakable end of these adaptations is the welfare of the animal or plant; they conduce to length and completeness of life, to the permanence and prosperity of the species. For some time, therefore, the arguments of natural theology seemed to be victorious along the whole line. The same kind of reasoning was pushed farther and farther to explain the classification and morphology of plants and animals; until the climax was reached in Agassiz's remarkable "Essay on Classification," published in 1859, in which every organic form was not only regarded as a concrete thought of the Creator interpretable by the human mind, but this kind of explanation was expressly urged as a substitute for inquiries into the physical causes whereby such forms might have been originated.

In its best days, however, there was a serious weakness in the argument from design, which was ably pointed out by Mr. Mill, in an essay wherein he accords much more weight to the general argument than could now by any possibility be granted it. Its fault was the familiar logical weakness of proving too much. The very success of the argument in showing the world to have been the work of an intelligent Designer made it impossible to suppose that Creator to be at once omnipotent and absolutely benevolent. For nothing can be clearer than that Nature is full of cruelty and maladaptation. In every part of the animal world we find implements of torture surpassing in devilish ingenuity anything that was ever seen in the dungeons of the Inquisition. We are introduced to a scene of incessant and universal strife, of which it is not apparent on the surface that the outcome is the good or the happiness of anything that is sentient. In pre-Darwinian times, before we had gone below the surface, no such outcome was discernible. Often, indeed, we find the higher life wantonly sacrificed to the lower, as instanced by the myriads of parasites apparently created for no other purpose than to prey upon creatures better than themselves. Such considerations bring up, with renewed emphasis, the ever-

The Idea of God.

lasting problem of the origin of evil. If the Creator of such a world is omnipotent he cannot be actuated solely by a desire for the welfare of his creatures, but must have other ends in view to which this is in some measure subordinated. Or if he is absolutely benevolent, then he cannot be omnipotent, but there is something in the nature of things which sets limits to his creative power. This dilemma is as old as human thinking, and it still remains a stumbling-block in the way of any theory of the universe that can possibly be devised. But it is an obstacle especially formidable to any kind of anthropomorphic theism. For the only avenue of escape is the assumption of an inscrutable mystery which would contain the solution of the problem if the human intellect could only penetrate so far; and the more closely we invite a comparison between divine and human methods of working, the more do we close up that only outlet.

The practical solution oftenest adopted

has been that which sacrifices the Creator's omnipotence in favour of his benevolence. In the noblest of the purely Aryan religions — that of which the sacred literature is contained in the Zendavesta — the evil spirit Ahriman exists independently of the will of the good Ormuzd, and is accountable for all the sin in the world, but in the fulness of time he is to be bound in chains and shorn of his power for mischief.[19] This theory has passed into Christendom in the form of Manichæism; but its essential features have been adopted by orthodox Christianity, which at the same time has tried to grasp the other horn of the dilemma and save the omnipotence of the Deity by paying him what Mr. Mill calls the doubtful compliment of making him the creator of the devil. By this device the essential polytheism of the conception is thinly veiled. The confusion of thought has been persistently blinked by the popular mind; but among the profoundest thinkers of the Aryan race there have been two who have explicitly adopted the solution which limits the Creator's power. One of these was Plato, who held that God's perfect goodness has been partially thwarted by the intractableness of the materials he has had to work with. This theory was carried to extremes by those Gnostics who believed that God's work consisted in redeeming a world originally created by the devil, and in orthodox Christianity it gave rise to the Augustinian doctrine of total depravity, and the "philosophy of the plan of salvation" founded thereon. The other great thinker who adopted a similar solution was Leibnitz. In his famous theory of optimism the world is by no means represented as perfect; it is only the best of all possible worlds, the best the Creator could make out of the materials at hand. In recent times Mr. Mill shows a marked preference for this view, and one of the foremost religious teachers now living, Dr. Martineau, falls into a parallel line of thinking in his suggestion that the primary qualities of matter constitute a "datum objective to God," who, "in shaping the orbits out of immensity, and determining seasons out of eternity, could but follow the laws of curvature, measure, and proportion."[20]

But indeed it is not necessary to refer to the problem of evil in order to show that the argument from design cannot prove the existence of an omnipotent and benevolent Designer. It is not omnipotence that contrives and plans and adapts means to ends. These are the methods of finite intelligence; they imply the overcoming of obstacles; and to ascribe them to omnipotence is to combine words that severally possess meanings into a phrase that has no meaning. "God said, Let there be light: and there was light." In this noble description of creative omnipotence one would search in vain for any hint of contrivance. The most the argument from design could legitimately hope to accomplish was to make it seem probable that the universe was wrought into its present shape by an intelligent and benevolent Being immeasurably superior to Man, but far from infinite in power and resources. Such an argument hardly rises to the level of true theism.[21]

X.

Simile of the Watch replaced by Simile of the Flower.

IT was in its own chosen stronghold that this once famous argument was destined to meet its doom. It was in the adaptations of the organic world, in the manifold harmonies between living creatures and surrounding circumstances, that it had seemed to find its chief support; and now came the Darwinian theory of natural selection, and in the twinkling of an eye knocked all this support from under it. It is not that the organism and its environment have been adapted to each other by an exercise of creative intelligence, but it is that the organism is necessarily fitted to the environment because in the perennial slaughter that has gone on from the beginning only the fittest have survived. Or, as it has been otherwise expressed, "the earth is suited to its inhabitants because it has produced them, and only such as suit it live." In the struggle for existence no individual peculiarity, however slight, that tends to the preservation of life is neglected. It is unerringly seized upon and propagated by natural selection, and from the cumulative action of such slight causes have come the beautiful adaptations of which the organic world is full. The demonstration of this point, through the labours of a whole generation of naturalists, has been one of the most notable achievements of modern science, and to the theistic arguments of Paley and the Bridgewater treatises it has dealt destruction.

But the Darwinian theory of natural selection does not stand alone. It is part of a greater whole. It is the most conspicuous portion of that doctrine of evolution in which all the results hitherto attained by the great modern scientific movement are codified, and which Herbert Spencer had already begun to set forth in its main outlines before the Darwinian theory had been made known to the world. This doctrine of evolution so far extends the range of our vision through past and future time as entirely to alter our conception of the universe. Our grandfathers, in common with all preceding generations of men, could and did suppose that at some particular moment in the past eternity the world was created in very much the shape which it has at present. But our modern knowledge does not allow us to suppose anything of the sort. We can carry back our thoughts through a long succession of great epochs, some of them many millions of years in duration, in each of which the innumerable forms of life that covered the earth were very different from what they were in all the others, and in even the nearest of which they were notably different from what they are now. We can go back still farther to the eras when the earth was a whirling ball of vapour, or when it formed an equatorial belt upon a sun two hundred million miles in diameter, or when the sun itself was but a giant nebula from which as yet no planet had been born. And through all the vast sweep of time, from the simple primeval vapour down to the multifarious world we know to-day, we see the various forms of Nature coming into existence one after the other in accordance with laws of which we are already beginning to trace the character and scope. Paley's simile of the watch is no longer applicable to such a world as this. It must be replaced by the simile of the flower. The universe is not a machine, but an organism, with an indwelling principle of life. It was not made, but it has grown.

That such a change in our conception of the universe marks the greatest revolution that has ever taken place in human thinking need scarcely be said. But even in this statement we have not quite revealed the depth of the change. Not only has modern science made it clear that the varied forms of Nature which make up the universe have arisen through a process of evolution, but it has also made it clear that what we call the laws of Nature have been evolved through the self-same process. The axiom of the persistence of force, upon which all modern science has come to rest, involves as a necessary corollary the persistence of the relations between forces; so that, starting with the persistence of force and the primary qualities of matter, it can be shown that all those uniformities of coexistence and succession which we call natural laws have arisen one after the other in connection with the forms which have afforded the occasions for their manifestation. The all-pervading harmony of Nature is thus itself a natural product, and the last inch of ground is cut away from under the theologians who suppose the universe to have come into existence through a supernatural process of manufacture at the hands of a Creator outside of itself.

XI.

The Craving for a Final Cause.

IT appears, then, that the idea of God as remote from the world is not likely to survive the revolution in thought which the rapid increase of modern knowledge has inaugurated. The knell of anthropomorphic or Augustinian theism has already sounded. This conclusion need not, however, disturb us when we consider how imperfect a form of theism this is which mankind is now outgrowing. To get rid of the appearance of antagonism between science and religion will of itself be one of the greatest benefits ever conferred upon the human race. It will forward science and purify religion, and it will go far toward increasing kindness and mutual helpfulness among men. Since such happy results are likely to follow the general adoption of the cosmic or Athanasian form of theism, in place of the other form, it becomes us to observe more specifically the manner in which this higher theism stands related to our modern knowledge.

To every form of theism, as I have already urged, an anthropomorphic element is indispensable. It is quite true, on the one hand, that to ascribe what we know as human personality to the infinite Deity straightway lands us in a contradiction, since personality without limits is inconceivable. But on the other hand, it is no less true that the total elimination of anthropomorphism from the idea of God abolishes the idea itself. This difficulty need not dishearten us, for it is no more than we must expect to encounter on the threshold of such a problem as the one before us. We do not approach the question in the spirit of those natural theologians who were so ready with their explanations of the divine purposes. We are aware that "we see as through a glass darkly," and we do not expect to "think God's thoughts after him" save in the crudest symbolic fashion. In dealing with the Infinite we are confessedly treating of that which transcends our powers of conception. Our ability to frame ideas is strictly limited by experience, and our experience does not furnish the materials for the idea of a personality which is not narrowly hemmed in by the inexorable barriers of circumstance. We therefore cannot conceive such an idea. But it does not follow that there is no reality answering to what such an idea would be if it could be conceived. The test of inconceivability is only applicable to the world of phenomena from which our experience is gathered. It fails when applied to that which lies behind phenomena. I do not hold for this reason that we are justified in using such an expression as "infinite personality" in a philosophical inquiry where clearness of thought and speech is above all things desirable. But I do hold, most emphatically, that we are not debarred from ascribing a quasi-psychical nature to the Deity simply because we can frame no proper conception of such a nature as absolute and infinite.

The point is of vital importance to theism. As Kant has well said, "the conception of God involves not merely a blindly operating Nature as the eternal root of things, but a Supreme Being that shall be the author of all things by free and understanding action; and it is this conception which alone has any interest for us." It will be observed that Kant says nothing here about "contrivance." By the phrase "free and understanding action" he doubtless means much the same that is here meant by ascribing to God a quasi-psychical nature. And thus alone, he says, can we feel any interest in theism. The thought goes deep, yet is plain enough to every one. The teleological instinct in Man cannot be suppressed or ignored.

The human soul shrinks from the thought that it is without kith or kin in all this wide universe. Our reason demands that there shall be a reasonableness in the constitution of things. This demand is a fact in our psychical nature as positive and irrepressible as our acceptance of geometrical axioms and our rejection of whatever controverts such axioms. No ingenuity of argument can bring us to believe that the infinite Sustainer of the universe will "put us to permanent intellectual confusion." There is in every earnest thinker a craving after a final cause; and this craving can no more be extinguished than our belief in objective reality. Nothing can persuade us that the universe is a farrago of nonsense. Our belief in what we call the evidence of our senses is less strong than our faith that in the orderly sequence of events there is a meaning which our minds could fathom were they only vast enough. Doubtless in our own age, of which it is a most healthful symptom that it questions everything, there are many who, through inability to assign the grounds for such a faith, have persuaded themselves that it must be a mere superstition which ought not to be cherished; but it is not likely that any one of these has ever really succeeded in ridding himself of it.

According to Mr. Spencer, the only ultimate test of reality is persistence, and the only measure of validity among our primary beliefs is the success with which they resist all efforts to change them. Let us see, then, how it is with the belief in the essential reasonableness of the universe. Does this belief answer to any outward reality? Is there, in the scheme of things, aught that justifies Man in claiming kinship of any sort with the God that is immanent in the world?

The difficulty in answering such questions has its root in the impossibility of framing a representative conception of Deity; but it is a difficulty which may, for all practical purposes, be surmounted by the aid of a symbolic conception.

XII.

Symbolic Conceptions.

OBSERVE the meaning of this distinction. Of any simple object which can be grasped in a single act of perception, such as a knife or a book, an egg or an orange, a circle or a triangle, you can frame a conception which almost or quite exactly *represents* the object. The picture or visual image in your mind when the orange is present to the senses is almost exactly reproduced when it is absent. The distinction between the two lies chiefly in the relative vividness of the former as contrasted with the relative faintness of the latter. But as the objects of thought increase in size and in complexity of detail, the case soon comes to be very different. You cannot frame a truly representative conception of the town in which you live, however familiar you may be with its streets and houses, its parks and trees, and the looks and demeanour of the townsmen; it is impossible to embrace so many details in a single mental picture. The mind must range to and fro among the phenomena in order to represent the town in a series of conceptions. But practically what you have in mind when you speak of the town is a fragmentary conception in which some portion of the object is represented, while you are well aware that with sufficient pains a series of mental pictures could be formed which would approximately correspond to the object. That is to say, this fragmentary conception stands in your mind as a *symbol* of the town. To some extent the conception is representative, but to a great degree it is symbolic. With a further increase in the size and complexity of the objects of thought, our conceptions gradually lose their representative character, and at length become purely symbolic. No one can form a mental picture that answers even approximately to the earth. Even a homogeneous ball eight thousand miles in diameter is too vast an object to be conceived otherwise than symbolically, and much more is this true of the ball upon which we live, with all its endless multiformity of detail. We imagine a globe and clothe it with a few terrestrial attributes, and in our minds this fragmentary notion does duty as a symbol of the earth.

The case becomes still more striking when we have to deal with conceptions of the universe, of cosmic forces such as light and heat, or of the stupendous secular changes which modern science calls us to contemplate. Here our conceptions cannot even pretend to represent the objects; they are as purely symbolic as the algebraic equations whereby the geometer expresses the shapes of curves. Yet so long as there are means of verification at our command, we can reason as safely with these symbolic conceptions as if they were truly representative. The geometer can at any moment translate his equation into an actual curve, and thereby test the results of his reasoning; and the case is similar with the undulatory theory of light, the chemist's conception of atomicity, and other vast stretches of thought which in recent times have revolutionized our knowledge of Nature. The danger in the use of symbolic conceptions is the danger of framing illegitimate symbols that answer to nothing in heaven or earth, as has happened first and last with so many short-lived theories in science and in metaphysics. Forewarned of this danger, and therefore — I hope — forearmed against it, let us see what a scientific philosophy has to say about the Power that is manifested in and through the universe.

XIII.

The Eternal Source of Phenomena.

WE have seen that before men could arrive at the idea of God, before out of the old crude and fragmentary polytheisms there could be developed a pure and coherent theism, it was necessary that physical generalization should have advanced far enough to enable them, however imperfectly, to reason about the universe as a whole. It was a faint glimpse of the unity of Nature that first led men to the conception of the unity of God, and as their knowledge of the phenomenal fact becomes clearer, so must their grasp upon the noumenal truth behind it become firmer. Now the whole tendency of modern science is to impress upon us ever more forcibly the truth that the entire knowable universe is an immense unit, animated throughout all its parts by a single principle of life. This conclusion, which was long ago borne in upon the minds of prophetic thinkers, like Spinoza and Goethe, through their keen appreciation of the significance of the physical harmonies known to them, has during the last fifty years received something like a demonstration in detail. It is since Goethe's death, for example, that it has been proved that the Newtonian law of gravitation extends to the bodies which used to be called fixed stars. That such was the case was already much more than probable, but so lately as 1835 there were to be found writers on science, such as Comte, who denied that it could ever be proved. But a still more impressive illustration of the unity of Nature is furnished by the luminiferous ether, when considered in connection with the discovery of the correlation of forces. The fathomless abysses of space can no longer be talked of as empty; they are filled with a wonderful substance, unlike any of the forms of matter which we can weigh and measure. A cosmic jelly almost infinitely hard and elastic, it offers at the same time no appreciable resistance to the movements of the heavenly bodies. It is so sensitive that a shock in any part of it causes a "tremour which is felt on the surface of countless worlds." Radiating in every direction, from millions of centric points, run shivers of undulation manifested in endless metamorphosis as heat, or light, or actinism, as magnetism or electricity. Crossing one another in every imaginable way, as if all space were crowded with a mesh-work of nerve-threads, these motions go on forever in a harmony that nothing disturbs. Thus every part of the universe shares in the life of all the other parts, as when in the solar atmosphere, pulsating at its temperature of a million degrees Fahrenheit, a slight breeze instantly sways the needles in every compass-box on the face of the earth.

Still further striking confirmation is found in the marvellous disclosures of spectrum analysis. To whatever part of the heavens we turn the telescope, armed with this new addition to our senses, we find the same chemical elements with which the present century has made us familiar upon the surface of the earth. From the distant worlds of Arcturus and the Pleiades, whence the swift ray of light takes many years to reach us, it brings the story of the hydrogen and oxygen, the vapour of iron or sodium, which set it in motion. Thus in all parts of the universe that have fallen within our ken we find a unity of chemical composition. Nebulæ, stars, and planets are all made of the same materials, and on every side we behold them in different stages of development, worlds in the making: here an irregular nebula such as our solar system once was, there a nebula whose rotation has at length wrought it into spheroidal form; here and there stars of varied colours marking different eras in chemical evolution; now planets still partly incandescent like Saturn and Jupiter, then planets like Mars and the earth, with cool atmospheres and solid continents and vast oceans of water; and lastly such bodies as the moon, vapourless, rigid, and cold in death.

Still nearer do we come toward realizing the unity of Nature when we recollect that the law of evolution is not only the same for all these various worlds, but is also the same throughout all other orders of phenomena. Not only in the development of cosmical bodies, including the earth, but also in the development of life upon the earth's surface and in the special development of those complex manifestations of life known as human societies, the most general and fundamental features of the process are the same, so that it has been found possible to express them in a single universal formula. And what is most striking of all, this notable formula, under which Herbert Spencer has succeeded in generalizing the phenomena of universal evolution, was derived from the formula under which Von Baer in 1829 first generalized the mode of development of organisms from their embryos. That a law of evolution first partially detected among the phenomena of the organic world should thereafter not only be found applicable to all other orders of phenomena, but should find in this application its first complete and coherent statement, is a fact of wondrous and startling significance. It means that the universe as a whole is thrilling in every fibre with Life, — not, indeed, life in the usual restricted sense, but life in a general sense. The distinction, once deemed absolute, between the living and the not-living is converted into a relative distinction; and Life as manifested in the organism is seen to be only a specialized form of the Universal Life.

The conception of matter as dead or inert belongs, indeed, to an order of thought that modern knowledge has entirely outgrown. If the study of physics has taught us anything, it is that nowhere in Nature is inertness or quiescence to be found. All is quivering with energy. From particle to particle without cessation the movement passes on, reappearing from moment to moment under myriad Protean forms, while the rearrangements of particles incidental to the movement constitute the qualitative differences among things. Now in the language of physics all motions of matter are manifestations of force, to which we can assign neither beginning nor end. Matter is indestructible, motion is continuous, and beneath both these universal truths lies the fundamental truth that force is persistent. The farthest reach in science that has ever been made was made when it was proved by Herbert Spencer that the law of universal evolution is a necessary consequence of the persistence of force. It has shown us that all the myriad phenomena of the universe, all its weird and subtle changes, in all their minuteness from moment to moment, in all their vastness from age to age, are the manifestations of a single animating principle that is both infinite and eternal.

By what name, then, shall we call this animating principle of the universe, this eternal source of phenomena? Using the ordinary language of physics, we have just been calling it Force, but such a term in no wise enlightens us. Taken by itself it is meaningless; it acquires its meaning only from the relations in which it is used. It is a mere symbol, like the algebraic expression which stands for a curve. Of what, then, is it the symbol?

The words which we use are so enwrapped in atmospheres of subtle associations that they are liable to sway the direction of our thoughts in ways of which we are often unconscious. It is highly desirable that physics should have a word as thoroughly abstract, as utterly emptied of all connotations of personality, as possible, so that it may be used like a mathematical symbol. Such a word is Force. But what we are now dealing with is by no means a scientific abstraction. It is the most concrete and solid of realities, the one Reality which underlies all appearances, and from the presence of which we can never escape. Suppose, then, that we translate our abstract terminology into something that is more concrete. Instead of the force which persists, let us speak of the Power which is always and everywhere manifested in phenomena. Our question, then, becomes, What is this infinite and eternal Power like? What kind of language shall we use in describing it? Can we regard it as in any wise "material," or can we speak of its universal and ceaseless activity as in any wise the working of a "blind necessity"? For here, at length, we have penetrated to the innermost kernel of the problem; and upon the answer must depend our mental attitude toward the mystery of existence.

The answer is that we cannot regard the infinite and eternal Power as in any wise "material," nor can we attribute its workings to "blind necessity." The eternal source of phenomena is the source of what we see and hear and touch; it is the source of what we call matter, but it cannot itself be material. Matter is but the generalized name we give to those modifications which we refer immediately to an unknown something outside of ourselves. It was long ago shown that all the qualities of matter are what the mind makes them, and have no existence as such apart from the mind. In the deepest sense all that we really know is mind, and as Clifford would say, what we call the material universe is simply an imperfect picture in our minds of a real universe of mind-stuff.[22] Our own mind we know directly; our neighbour's mind we know by inference; that which is external to both is a Power hidden from sense, which causes states of consciousness that are similar in both.

Such states of consciousness we call material qualities, and matter is nothing but the sum of such qualities. To speak of the hidden Power itself as "material" is therefore not merely to state what is untrue, — it is to talk nonsense. We are bound to conceive of the Eternal Reality in terms of the only reality that we know, or else refrain from conceiving it under any form whatever. But the latter alternative is clearly impossible.[23] We might as well try to escape from the air in which we breathe as to expel from consciousness the Power which is manifested throughout what we call the material universe. But the only conclusion we can consistently hold is that this is the very same power "which in ourselves wells up under the form of consciousness."

In the nature-worship of primitive men, beneath all the crudities of thought by which it was overlaid and obscured, there was thus after all an essential germ of truth which modern philosophy is constrained to recognize and reiterate. As the unity of Nature has come to be demonstrated, innumerable finite powers, once conceived as psychical and deified, have been generalized into a single infinite Power that is still thought of as psychical. From the crudest polytheism we have thus, by a slow evolution, arrived at pure monotheism, — the recognition of the eternal God indwelling in the universe, in whom we live and move and have our being.

But in thus conceiving of God as psychical, as a Being with whom the human soul in the deepest sense owns kinship, we must beware of too carelessly ascribing to Him those specialized psychical attributes characteristic of humanity, which one and all imply limitation and weakness. We must not forget the warning of the prophet Isaiah: "My thoughts are not your thoughts, neither are your ways my ways, saith the Lord. For as the heavens are higher than the earth, so are my ways higher than your ways, and my thoughts than your thoughts." Omniscience, for example, has been ascribed to God in every system of theism; yet the psychical nature to which all events, past, present, and future, can be always simultaneously present is clearly as far removed from the limited and serial psychical nature of Man as the heavens are higher than the earth. We are not so presumptuous, therefore, as to attempt, with some theologians of the anthropomorphic school, to inquire minutely into the character of the divine decrees and purposes. But our task would be ill-performed were nothing more to be said about that craving after a final cause which we have seen to be an essential element in Man's religious nature. It remains to be shown that there is a reasonableness in the universe, that in the orderly sequence of events there is a meaning which appeals to our human intelligence. Without adopting Paley's method, which has been proved inadequate, we may nevertheless boldly aim at an object like that at which Paley aimed. Caution is needed, since we are dealing with a symbolic conception as to which the very point in question is whether there is any reality that answers to it. The problem is a hard one, but here we suddenly get powerful help from the doctrine of evolution, and especially from that part of it known as the Darwinian theory.

XIV.

The Power that makes for Righteousness.

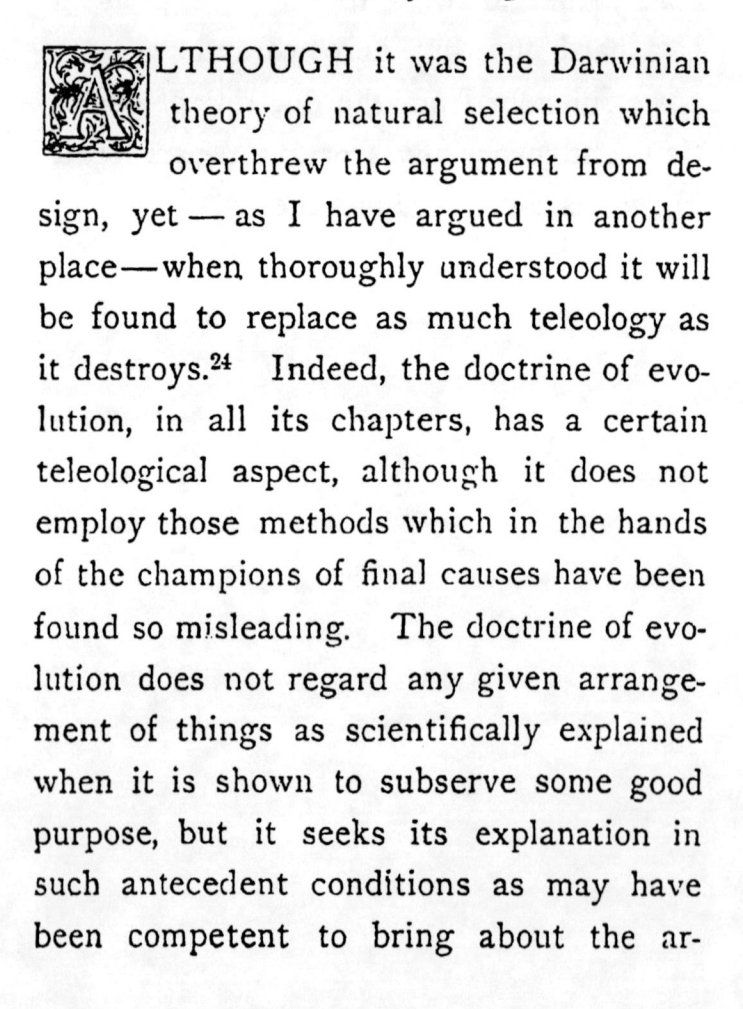

ALTHOUGH it was the Darwinian theory of natural selection which overthrew the argument from design, yet — as I have argued in another place — when thoroughly understood it will be found to replace as much teleology as it destroys.[24] Indeed, the doctrine of evolution, in all its chapters, has a certain teleological aspect, although it does not employ those methods which in the hands of the champions of final causes have been found so misleading. The doctrine of evolution does not regard any given arrangement of things as scientifically explained when it is shown to subserve some good purpose, but it seeks its explanation in such antecedent conditions as may have been competent to bring about the ar-

The Idea of God. 159

rangement in question. Nevertheless, the doctrine of evolution is not only perpetually showing us the purposes which the arrangements of Nature subserve, but throughout one large section of the ground which it covers it points to a discernible dramatic tendency, a clearly-marked progress of events toward a mighty goal. Now it especially concerns us to note that this large section is just the one, and the only one, which our powers of imagination are able to compass. The astronomic story of the universe is altogether too vast for us to comprehend in such wise as to tell whether it shows any dramatic tendency or not.[25] But in the story of the evolution of life upon the surface of our earth, where alone we are able to compass the phenomena, we see all things working together, through countless ages of toil and trouble, toward one glorious consummation. It is therefore a fair inference, though a bold one, that if our means of exploration were such that we could compass the story of all the systems of worlds that shine in the spacious firmament, we should be able to detect a similar meaning. At all events, the story which we can decipher is sufficiently impressive and consoling. It clothes our theistic belief with moral significance, reveals the intense and solemn reality of religion, and fills the heart with tidings of great joy.

The glorious consummation toward which organic evolution is tending is the production of the highest and most perfect psychical life. Already the germs of this conclusion existed in the Darwinian theory as originally stated, though men were for a time too busy with other aspects of the theory to pay due attention to them. In the natural selection of such individual peculiarities as conduce to the survival of the species, and in the evolution by this process of higher and higher creatures endowed with capacities for a richer and more varied life, there might have been

The Idea of God. 161

seen a well-marked dramatic tendency, toward the *dénouement* of which every one of the myriad little acts of life and death during the entire series of geologic æons was assisting. The whole scheme was teleological, and each single act of natural selection had a teleological meaning. Herein lies the reason why the theory so quickly destroyed that of Paley. It did not merely refute it, but supplanted it with explanations which had the merit of being truly scientific, while at the same time they hit the mark at which natural theology had unsuccessfully aimed.

Such was the case with the Darwinian theory as first announced. But since it has been more fully studied in its application to the genesis of Man, a wonderful flood of light has been thrown upon the meaning of evolution, and there appears a reasonableness in the universe such as had not appeared before. It has been shown that the genesis of Man was due to a change in the direction of the working of natural selection, whereby psychical variations were selected to the neglect of physical variations. It has been shown that one chief result of this change was the lengthening of infancy, whereby Man appeared on the scene as a plastic creature capable of unlimited psychical progress. It has been shown that one chief result of the lengthening of infancy was the origination of the family and of human society endowed with rudimentary moral ideas and moral sentiments. It has been shown that through these cooperating processes the difference between Man and all lower creatures has come to be a difference in kind transcending all other differences; that his appearance upon the earth marked the beginning of the final stage in the process of development, the last act in the great drama of creation; and that all the remaining work of evolution must consist in the perfecting of the creature thus marvellously produced. It has been further shown that the perfecting of Man consists mainly in the ever-increasing predominance of the life of the soul over the life of the body. And lastly, it has been shown that, whereas the earlier stages of human progress have been characterized by a struggle for existence like that through which all lower forms of life have been developed, nevertheless the action of natural selection upon Man is coming to an end, and his future development will be accomplished through the direct adaptation of his wonderfully plastic intelligence to the circumstances in which it is placed. Hence it has appeared that war and all forms of strife, having ceased to discharge their normal function, and having thus become unnecessary, will slowly die out;[26] that the feelings and habits adapted to ages of strife will ultimately perish from disuse; and that a stage of civilization will be reached in which human sympathy shall be all in all, and the spirit of Christ shall reign supreme throughout the length and breadth of the earth.

These conclusions, with the grounds upon which they are based, have been succinctly set forth in my little book entitled "The Destiny of Man viewed in the Light of his Origin." Startling as they may have seemed to some, they are no more so than many of the other truths which have been brought home to us during this unprecedented age. They are the fruit of a wide induction from the most vitally important facts which the doctrine of evolution has set forth; and they may fairly claim recognition as an integral body of philosophic doctrine fit to stand the test of time. Here they are summarized as the final step in my argument concerning the true nature of theism. They add new meanings to the idea of God, as it is affected by modern knowledge, while at the same time they do but give articulate voice to time-honoured truths which it was feared the skepticism of our age might have rendered dumb and powerless. For if we express in its most concentrated form the meaning of these conclusions regarding Man's origin and destiny, we find that it affords the full justification of the fundamental ideas and sentiments which have animated religion at all times. We see Man still the crown and glory of the universe and the chief object of divine care, yet still the lame and halting creature, loaded with a brute-inheritance of original sin, whose ultimate salvation is slowly to be achieved through ages of moral discipline. We see the chief agency which produced him — natural selection which always works through strife — ceasing to operate upon him, so that, until human strife shall be brought to an end, there goes on a struggle between his lower and his higher impulses, in which the higher must finally conquer. And in all this we find the strongest imaginable incentive to right living, yet one that is still the same in principle with that set forth by the great Teacher who first brought men to the knowledge of the true God.

As to the conception of Deity, in the shape impressed upon it by our modern knowledge, I believe I have now said enough to show that it is no empty formula or metaphysical abstraction which we would seek to substitute for the living God. The infinite and eternal Power that is manifested in every pulsation of the universe is none other than the living God. We may exhaust the resources of metaphysics in debating how far his nature may fitly be expressed in terms applicable to the psychical nature of Man; such vain attempts will only serve to show how we are dealing with a theme that must ever transcend our finite powers of conception. But of some things we may feel sure. Humanity is not a mere local incident in an endless and aimless series of cosmical changes. The events of the universe are not the work of chance, neither are they the outcome of blind necessity. Practically there is a purpose in the world whereof it is our highest duty to learn the lesson, however well or ill we may fare in rendering a scientific account of it. When from the dawn of life we see all things working together toward the evolution of the highest spiritual attributes of Man, we know, however the words may stumble in which we try to say it, that God is in the deepest sense a moral Being. The everlasting source of phenomena is none other than the infinite Power that makes for righteousness. Thou canst not by searching find Him out; yet put thy trust in Him, and against thee the gates of hell shall not prevail; for there is neither wisdom nor understanding nor counsel against the Eternal.

NOTES.

A.—MEDITATIONS OF A SAVAGE.

In the presence of the great mystery of existence, the thoughts of the untutored savage are not always so very unlike those of civilized men, as we may see from the following pathetic words of a Kafir, named Sekese, in conversation with a French traveller, M. Arbrouseille, on the subject of the Christian religion:—

"Your tidings," said this uncultivated barbarian, "are what I want, and I was seeking before I knew you, as you shall hear and judge for yourself. Twelve years ago I went to feed my flocks; the weather was hazy. I sat down upon a rock and asked myself sorrowful questions; yes, sorrowful, because I was unable to answer them. Who has touched the stars with his hands — on what pillars do they rest, I asked myself. The waters never weary, they know no other law than to flow without ceasing from morning till night and from night till morning; but where do they stop, and who makes them flow thus? The clouds also come and go, and burst in water over the earth. Whence come they — who sends them? The diviners certainly do not give us rain; for how could they do it? and why do not I see them with my own eyes when they go up to heaven to fetch it? I cannot see the wind; but what is it? who brings it, makes it blow and roar and terrify us? Do I know how the corn sprouts? Yesterday there was not a blade in my field, to-day I returned to the field and found some; who can have given to the earth the wisdom and the power to produce it? Then I buried my head in both my hands." — Cited in PICTON, *Mystery of Matter*, p. 222.

B. — THE NAME *GOD*.

NONE of the dictionaries offer a satisfactory explanation of the word *God*. It was once commonly supposed to be related to the adjective *good*, but Grimm long ago showed that this connection is, to say the least, very improbable. It has also been sought to identify it with Persian *Khodâ*, from Zend *qvadata*, Skr. *svadata*, Lat. *a se datus*, in which the idea is that of self-existence; but this fanciful etymology was exploded by Aufrecht. The arrant guesswork of Donaldson, who would connect *God* with καλός, and θεός with τίθημι (New Cratylus, p. 710), scarcely deserves mention in these days. Among the more scientific philologists of our time, August Fick, in treating of the "Wortschatz der germanischen Spracheinheit," simply refers *God* to a primitive Teutonic *gutha*, and says no more about it. (Vergl. Woerterbuch der indogermanischen Sprachen, III. 107.) He is followed by Skeat (Etymological Dictionary, p. 238), who adds that there is "no connection with *good*." Eduard Müller says: "So bedenklich die zusammenstellung mit *good*, so fraglich ist doch auch noch die urverwandtschaft mit pers. *Khodâ* gott, oder skr. *gûdha* mysterium, oder skr. *guddha* purus; Heyne: 'als sich verhüllender, unsichtbarer, vgl. skr. *guh* für *gudh* celare.'" (Woerterbuch der englischen Sprache, p. 456.)

Max Müller has much more plausibly suggested that *God* was formerly a heathen name for the Deity, which passed into Christian usage, like the Latin *Deus*. (Science of Language, 6th ed. II. 317.) Following this hint, I suggested, several years ago (North Amer. Review, Oct. 1869, p. 354), that *God* is probably identical with *Wodan* or *Odin*, the name of the great Northern deity, the chief object of the worship of our forefathers. This relation of an initial *G* to an initial *W* is a very common one; as for example *Guillaume* and *William*, *guerre* and *war*, *guardian* and *warden*, *guile* and *wile*. The same thing is seen in Armorican *guasta* and Ital. *guastare*, as compared with Lat. *vastare*, Eng. *waste;* and in the Eng. *quick*, Goth. *quivs*, Lat. *vivus*. In Erchempert's Historia Langobardorum, 11, Pertz, III. 245, we find *Ludoguicus* for *Ludovicus*. Not only is this relation a common one, but there are plenty of specific instances of it in the case of *Wodan*. In Germany we have the town names of *Godesberg, Gudenberg,* and *Godensholt,* all derived from *Wodan*. In the Westphalian dialect, *Wednesday* ("day of Wodan") is called *Godenstag* or *Gunstag;* in Nether-Rhenish, *Gudenstag;* in Flemish, *Goenstag.* See Thorpe, Northern Mythol. I. 229; Taylor, Words and Places, 323; and cf. Grimm, Gesch. der deutschen Sprache, 296. The Westphalian Saxons wrote both *Guodan* and *Gudan*. *Odin* was also called *Godin* (Laing, Heimskringla, I. 74), and Paulus Diaconus tells us that the Lombards pronounced *Wodan* as *Guodan*. In view of such a convergence of proofs, I am surprised that attention was not long ago called to this etymology.

Wodan was originally the storm-spirit or animating genius of the wind, answering in many respects to the Greek Hermes and the Vedic Sarameyas. See my Myths and Myth-makers, 19, 20, 32, 35, 67, 124, 204; and cf. Mackay, Religious Development of the Greeks and Hebrews, i. 260–273.

REFERENCES.

M. M., Myths and Myth-makers, 1872; C. P., Outlines of Cosmic Philosophy, 1874; U. W., The Unseen World, 1876; D., Darwinism and Other Essays, 1879; E. E., Excursions of an Evolutionist, 1884; D. M., The Destiny of Man, 1884; A. P. I., American Political Ideas, 1885.

1. E. E. 56–77.
2. C. P. i. 230.
3. C. P. i. 157, 177–179.
4. M. M. 18–21, *et passim*.
5. M. M. 220.
6. M. M. 232.
7. M. M. 236; E. E, 251.
8. A. P. I. 78, 81.
9. U. W. 10.
10. D. M. 104–107.
11. E. E. 262.
12. M. M. 236.
13. C. P. ii. 383.
14. U. W. 118.
15. D. 5–8; C. P. ii. 283.
16, 17. C. P. ii. 428.
18. C. P. i. 183; ii. 449.

19. M. M. 122.
20. C. P. ii. 405.
21. C. P. ii. 381–410.
22. E. E. 327–336.
23. C. P. ii. 449.
24. D. M. 113; cf. C. P. ii. 406.
25. D. 103.
26. D. M. 77–95; A. P. I. 101–152.

Printed in the United States
102294LV00003B/167/A